Attention Please! God Is Speaking!

Attention Please! God Is Speaking!

David C. Shultz

Warner Press, Inc.
Anderson, Indiana

All scripture passages, unless otherwise indicated,
are from the Holy Bible, New International Version.
Copyright ©1973, 1978,1984 International Bible Society.
Used by permission of Zondervan Bible Publishers.

© 1994 by Warner Press, Inc.
ISBN #0–87162–671–3   Stock #D2505
UPC 7–30817–22206–6

David C. Shultz, Editor in Chief
Dan Harman, Book Editor
Cover by John Silvey

This book is
lovingly dedicated to
Karon, Mimi, Jodi, and Jon
who teach me so much about
Christlike living.

Contents

x

Introduction

Few scriptures match the grandeur or depth of Hebrews 1:1 and 2, which declare, "In the past God spoke to our forefathers through the prophets at many times and in various ways, but in these last days he has spoken to us by his son. All of Hebrews soars and inspires, giving us some of our most meaningful verses and enduring concepts of God; for example, "Jesus Christ, the same yesterday, today, and forever" (Heb. 13:8). Small wonder that the 1994 convention program committee chose this book as a basis for the 1994 convention theme, "Attention, Please! God Is Speaking!"

This book is designed with two audiences in mind. Its first purpose is to enhance the experience of convention goers to the 1994 International Convention of the Church of God. Second, it is created to be read and studied quite apart from the convention, as a book to inspire Christian devotion.

The format simply follows the theme for each day of the convention, one for each of seven days. Those attending the convention can read additional inspirational material on each subject, each day. However, non-convention readers will not have to depend on the events or memories of the convention to enjoy the book. Unlike last year's theme book, we have not incorporated thoughts or comments from the various convention speakers, themselves.

Because of our thematic approach, no attempt will be made to study the book of Hebrews chronologically or exegetically.

Questions are provided at the conclusion of each chapter for study or discussion.

My prayer is that God will reveal himself to you through these pages.

Dear Father,

You have hounded us since before we were born because you love us. You have spoken through nature, people, and most eloquently through Jesus Christ. Speak to us today with the freshness of creation and the power of the resurrection, we pray. Amen.

1

Attention Please! God Is Speaking!

Hebrews 1:1–3; 2:1

People are frantic to hear from God. They often do not know it is God they are seeking, but they want to hear from someone, from some personality who can make sense out of life and death. Underneath the thin veneer of business as usual, there is a vast interest in reincarnation and communication with those who have died. One of America's most popular movies of the last ten years is *Ghost,* in which the skills of a reluctant medium are used to communicate between two lovers, one of whom was murdered. A recent television special documented the thousands of people who claim to talk regularly with angels. "Near death experiences" have lodged themselves in the popular mind and are more readily believed than Scripture.

Amazingly, it is socially acceptable to embrace the occult, but not to talk with God. For reasons too many and complex to list, Christianity and Jesus Christ are viewed by North Americans as less and less credible. As tragic as this may be, it is more tragic that many Christians themselves have lost any sense of personal relationship with God.

Some time ago at a ministers' meeting, I recounted how my son, Jonathan, encountered God personally when he was seven years old. His experience was so startling that our whole family was deeply affected, and I myself was shocked into reassessing and renewing my own relationship with God.[1] One sad looking pastor

3

later asked me, his voice tinged with hope, "Are you saying that it is possible to actually talk with God, personally?"

Yes! That's exactly what I'm saying. This is the eternal message of Scripture. "In the past God spoke to our forefathers through the prophets at many times and in various ways, but in these last days he has spoken to us by his Son, whom he appointed heir of all things, and through whom he made the universe. The Son is the radiance of God's glory and the exact representation of his being, sustaining all things by his powerful word."[2] The Hound of Heaven won't stop seeking us.

GOD IS NOT SILENT

God speaks in thousands of ways. Since the thrust of Hebrews 1:1–3 is to immediately highlight the surpassing person and ministry of Jesus Christ, there is only the briefest of allusions to God's incessant and eloquent self-revelations. What are some of the "many times and various ways God spoke to our forefathers"?

GOD SPEAKS THROUGH CREATION

Creation has always been one of God's most articulate voices. The glory and magnitude of the heavens, for example, provided a ceaseless reminder of God's greatness and wisdom to biblical writers.

When I consider your heavens, the work of your fingers,
    the moon and the stars, which you have set in place,
    what is man that you are mindful of him,
    the son of man that you care for him?[3]
O LORD my God, you are very great;
    you are clothed with splendor and majesty.
He wraps himself in light as with a garment;
    he stretches out the heavens like a tent
    and lays the beams of his upper chambers
        on their waters.
He makes the clouds his chariot
    and rides on the wings of the wind.
He makes winds his messengers, flames of fire his servants.[4]

On a more contemporary note, we read in the last few years about the interplanetary journeys of the space probe Voyager. In *National Geographic* we saw fantastic photographs of distant planets taken by Voyager's cameras. A monstrous, sullen Jupiter glared across the miles, hugging its scores of moons to itself like its own solar system. Neptune and Uranus glimmered like phantoms of blue green. But my favorite was Saturn. As I remember the commentary, the author recounted how Voyager had discovered enough about that one planet to keep astronomers puzzling for years. The rings are composed far differently than scientists had supposed. One of them even appears somehow braided. Such discoveries stretch what we know of the laws of matter and physics, and our most brilliant scholars are left scratching their heads. I don't know if this does anything for you, but it leads me to worship. No matter how sophisticated our instruments become at measuring the universe, God will be way out ahead of us.

The immutability and transcendence of nature becomes a defense of God's character in the Book of Job. The message seems to be that, with creation's overwhelming display of brilliance and power, there should be no question about God's existence, ability, or intent. After Job and his three friends exhausted their thimble-sized reservoir of God–knowledge, the Almighty spoke out of the storm.

He said:
"Who is this that darkens my counsel
    with words without knowledge?
"Brace yourself like a man;
    I will question you,
    and you shall answer me.
"Where were you when I laid the earth's foundation?
    Tell me, if you understand.
"Who marked off its dimensions? Surely you know!
    Who stretched a measuring line across it?
"On what were its footings set,
    or who laid its cornerstone—
    while the morning stars sang together
    and all the angels shouted for joy?

5

"Who shut up the sea behind doors
    when it burst forth from the womb ...
when I said, "This far you may come and no farther;
    here is where your proud waves halt"?
"Have you ever given orders to the morning,
    or shown the dawn its place...?
"Have you entered the storehouses of the snow...?
"What is the way to the place where the lightning is dispersed..?
"Can you raise your voice to the clouds
    and cover yourself with a flood of water?
"Do you send the lightning bolts on their way?
"Do they report to you, 'Here we are'?"[5]

Creation is compelling. God talks and teaches through just about anything. Sometimes humorously. Gerald Marvel, pastor of the First Church of God in Vancouver, Washington, tells of an early pastorate he had in Louisiana. He said that when he candidated the church leaders told him their priority was to get into a new building. He said that seemed an odd number one priority to him until he saw the old termite infested facility. So they stepped out on faith and contracted with an architect to draw a set of plans. They developed a three-year plan to raise funds, build, and be in their new facility. At the end of three years, the only thing that had happened was that they were behind on payments to the architect. It certainly was a discouraging time for a young pastor.

One Saturday night he was driving home late from performing a wedding somewhere up north. He stopped to get gas and was drinking coffee from a Styrofoam cup when he looked up and saw the beautiful night sky. He began to talk to God, first in praise for the beauty of the night. But, as he began to reflect, he thought about the speed of the light from those stars: 186,000 miles per second. "You know," he thought to himself, "that's seven times around the world before you can count 'one thousand one': faster than anything in creation except gossip in the church."

Then his praise changed to complaint. "God," he muttered, "if you can get light to me from those distant stars you created at 186,000 miles per second, why can't you move my church off dead center?" God was silent.

6

Later that night on his drive home he passed signs advertising caverns. God then spoke to Gerald. "You know, Gerald, millions of years ago I formed those caverns. They were, at first, huge underground holes with nothing of interest except size. One day I caused a drop of water to seep down through the rock formations and hang for a moment from the ceiling of those vacant caves. It dropped to the floor and ran away to join an underground river. It left the tiniest of rings, both on the ceiling and on the floor below. It would have taken a microscope to see the first ring. Bit by bit, drip by drip, over millions of years, I built those beautiful caverns." Pastor Marvel thought for a moment and then a single phrase summed up the experience.

"Gerald, I have you on my drip plan."[6]

GOD SPEAKS THROUGH MIRACLES

Even more than in creation, God's people gloried in the times he transcended natural law. These were the mile markers of the Hebrew experience. These were the "Ebenezers" where altars were built and memorial stones were erected. The events surrounding such supernatural manifestations were immortalized in songs and passed down from generation to generation. Here was proof that God not only existed, but acted on behalf of those who loved him.

Psalm 105 is a diary of these mile markers. This incredibly positive account mentions Israel's major moments, glorifies God, and overlooks all the complaints, disobedience, and pettiness so characteristic of his people. The psalm begins,

Give thanks to the Lord, call on his name;
    make known among the nations what he has done …
Remember the wonders he has done,
    his miracles, and the judgments he pronounced.

The writer then parades all the big events: the covenant with Abraham and the miracle son, Isaac, the journey to Egypt of Joseph and his meteoric rise to power, the calling of Moses and Aaron and the miraculous signs against Pharaoh, and the marvelous preservation of God's people in the wilderness.

7

In Acts 7, Stephen delivered an impassioned and inspired speech to the Sanhedrin. He, like the psalmist, recounted the milestones and miracles. Unlike the psalmist, he concluded that the miracles and signs were specific communication from God that his people rejected. His stinging conclusion: the refusal to hear God's voice led them to crucify Jesus Christ. Stephen's martyrdom was a final, eloquent illustration of the very truth he was trying to communicate. Signs and wonders are never free floating, granted for their own ability to evoke awe and wonder. They always come to communicate a greater lesson.

A Contemporary Case Study

Does God speak through miracles today? You be the judge.

In 1982 my wife, Karon, and I accepted the call to pastor North Anderson Church of God in Anderson, Indiana. The congregation had been started in 1906 by workers from the Gospel Trumpet home across town. For more than seventy-five years the church had built a strong and meaningful reputation in the community. They had endured some difficult days with prodigal leadership and were poised to chart a new course. They worshiped in a lovely brick facility, built in stages. The sanctuary, seating around three hundred, had been built in the 1950s. The educational unit, one of the finest I have seen anywhere, had been dedicated in 1970. Attendance was running around 450 on Sunday mornings. To be called to pastor this congregation was a great opportunity.

At our very first interview, one young leader asked the question, "What would you do if we had too many people for two morning services?" For more than fifteen years the congregation had used the two-service format on Sunday mornings, and everybody loved it. It allowed for flexibility of schedule and room to grow. To outgrow two services had not even crossed my mind. This question was a providential hint of what God had planned but few of us had imagined. As I recall, my answer was a feeble, "Well, we'll cross that bridge if and when we come to it."

In less than a year it became apparent that God was blessing us in an unusual way. Morning worship attendance jumped to more than six hundred, straining our space and abilities to cope. Our

Long Range Planning Committee had not entirely been taken by surprise, and they dusted off their proposals. One by one they proved unfeasible. Add to the balcony: too expensive. Knock out a wall in the sanctuary: structurally impractical. All the while attendance grew, forcing some temporary solution. Three services was the answer. We didn't know of many congregations who had tried it, but planned a schedule and struck out into unexplored territory.

Half way through our three-morning-service year, we were again packing them in. Attendance was now pushing an average of eight hundred. We set up ropes to restrain people waiting for the third service. Otherwise they crowded against the doors and second-service people couldn't exit. It was not unusual for the crowds to stretch out the door and down the street to the corner.

What to do? In another short-term measure, we voted to worship—as a one-year experiment—in a high school auditorium. We would never come back. The high school years tested our resolve and creativity. Many congregations have used schools, and they know what it's like to set up and tear down every week. My hat's off to all of them, especially those who keep at it year after year.

The Property

In 1985 the search for property began in earnest. We were not prepared for how difficult it would be. There was, of course, farmland. What we could afford was inaccessible or undesirable. Property on major highways was prohibitively expensive. The fact was, there wasn't much of anything, period. One parcel of land, about nineteen acres, was ideally situated but had two strikes against it. The land fell away from the road into a ravine, which we knew would make building difficult, perhaps impossible. Second, it was tied up in court and was simply not available.

We finally settled on seventeen acres at the intersection of two major thoroughfares. The price would stretch our resources, but was amazingly reasonable: $140,000. But the day before the business meeting in which we voted to relocate, that property was sold—to another church!

Time was running out and our options were spotty at best. We pushed ahead on two adjoining lots too far north of town, when

Chuck Staley, chair of our building committee, called on a whim about the property locked up in probate court.

"Mr. Staley, you're not going to believe this. The property you're asking about was released for sale this very afternoon."

"Really? What is your asking price?"

"$50,000."

This was too good to believe! Nineteen acres for almost two-thirds less money than seventeen acres? In a better location? We put money on the land that afternoon. We would later discover, when the land was surveyed, we had bought almost twenty-three acres, not nineteen.

Church Buildings: Selling the Old and Financing for New

This miracle energized our congregation in ways you can hardly imagine. But we had many more hurdles to cross. One of them was the sale of the church building we were leaving. Like any place you've lived for a while, it was comfortable and seemed very valuable to us. We were unprepared for the glum assessment local realtors gave us. Our faith was not their faith. Their comments still hiss in my ears.

"Church property isn't selling in central Indiana."

"Churches aren't selling in Indianapolis, let alone in Anderson."

"The most you could hope to get for this building is eleven cents per square foot."

"Perhaps you can use the building for some other purpose."

An independent appraisal had confirmed our realtors' melancholy dirge: $250,000 for the church building, property, plus a five-bedroom parsonage a block away! (We were insuring the place for 1.3 million dollars!) If we could just get $495,000 for it, we thought, we'd be well on our way toward that new building.

The realtors and building committee members went home. I walked slowly down the hallway to the small building next door that housed our church offices. Seldom had I been so discouraged. As I turned the corner to exit through the double doors, my eyes caught at something white on the outside window ledge. It was a white dove.

A white dove? In winter? In Indiana? At that moment I sensed God speaking. "It's a sign," God said. "Go outside and look at it. It won't leave or fly away."

I carefully approached the waist-high window ledge where the snowy bird sat, his head bobbing as he looked at me. "This dove will stay here for two days," God said, "as a sign that my Spirit is resting on this congregation. Our realtor friends are fine businessmen, but they don't know what I can do."

I hurried into the office and called Marge, our office manager. "Marge," I blurted, "come look at this! There's a white dove outside on the window ledge." As she hurried around her desk and out to the window, I told her what God had said. Sure enough, the dove sat quietly, looking at us inquisitively. Marge and I rushed in to get Wes, the associate pastor. We told him the story while all three of us dashed outside. There it sat, quite peacefully. The question was, would it be here the rest of the day? And would it be there tomorrow?

Early the next morning I drove to church. I didn't know what the chances were of a strange bird staying on one window sill for two days, but it didn't seem very likely to me. The first thing I saw when I pulled into the parking lot was the white dove. If it had moved, it wasn't obvious. My heart and spirit soared at the sight of that little bird. "For two days," God had said. On the third day, the dove was gone.

If I recall correctly, it was then that two things happened. The first was that our financing for the new church fell through. The bank that had assured us on several occasions that they would loan us the money to build reneged. When we announced this news on a Sunday morning, there was an audible gasp throughout the auditorium, as though some great balloon were losing air. Immediately the altars filled with people as they came to pray. Following the service a young seminarian slipped a note in my hand. He had scrawled these startling words on the torn-off corner of the church bulletin, "The Lord says, 'I will give you a better deal in the spring.'"

The second thing was that we started a weekly twenty-four-hour prayer vigil. The congregation was still marvelously infected by the property miracle. I don't think I had told the story of the dove at that time, (probably because I wanted to reserve some small bit of respect in their eyes as a rational leader who still had full use of his faculties). In any case, since we still had use of the old building, we proclaimed that Tuesdays were Days of Prayer, from 6:00 A.M. on Tuesday morning through the night to 6:00 A.M. on Wednesdays. We challenged the congregation to leave home and come to the church to pray. Yes, even in the middle of the night! But would anyone come out to pray? I wondered.

The first Day of Prayer more than two hundred people turned out! H. L. and Sandy Baker set their alarm for 3:00 A.M., hauled themselves out of the sack, and drove to the church in the snow. They found a group of enthusiastic people and college students banding together in prayer in the dead of night. Others told similar stories. Week after week hundreds came to pray. Countless others prayed at home.

There's so much about prayer I don't understand. Everyone who participated in those Days of Prayer was driven and energized. We were not only encouraged by the terrific turnout at the old building, we were buoyed up by the way God began working.

A gentleman from Fisher-Guide, a division of General Motors, telephoned me at the office. He was a member of Park Place Church of God, and had heard about our desire to sell the old church building. He said they wanted to develop a training center somewhere in town. So we set up a meeting with their plant managers. Week after week the meetings continued, with higher and higher levels of GM brass showing up. When the GM plane flew in people from Detroit, I knew we were on the home stretch.

The bombshell they dropped was that, the day before they were going to ink the deal, Detroit had issued a ruling that disallowed the purchase of any land or building not contiguous with already owned land. That, as they say, was that.

The days of prayer continued. Within a few days our Park Place friend called back. "Have you considered leasing the property?" he asked. No, I said, but we would be glad to. I quickly called Chuck Staley on the phone and he did some fast figuring. We came up with a proposal, presented it, hammered out the details in a couple of meetings, and bingo, the church was leased. It wasn't a sale, but then, it was better than nothing. Looking back on it ten years later, we couldn't have dreamed up a better scenario. If we had sold the building we would have gained $495,000. But in lease money, the congregation to this date has realized more than $1.2 million in income, and they still own the building!

Whatever happened to the financing? Well, my young seminary friend was right. Months before we had submitted a proposal to several local banks, including Citizens Banking Company. We had never heard any response from them, and had assumed they were not interested. In the spring, just as his scribbled note announced, God gave us a better deal. The vice-president of Citizen's Banking Company called and said, "Your loan is approved." Just like that!

What's the Message of These Miracles?

To remember the ways God worked during those challenging years always lifts my faith. I'm pretty sure all those who were there at the time would agree the same is true for them. But is this God's only purpose? No. Thousands have now heard this story. Scores have told me how their own faith has been reborn. One young pastor and his wife moved clear across the country and planted a new church because of this story. Perhaps there are others. One thing's certain: God is speaking today.

GOD SPEAKS THROUGH PEOPLE

People are some of God's favorite megaphones. Especially some people. The writer of Hebrews says "*through the prophets* at many times and in various ways" (italics added). The Old Testament is packed with prophets from the patriarchs like Abraham to the wild-eyed seers like Ezekiel. In the New Testament we have John the Baptist, who closes out the grand tradition and style of prophets in the Old Testament mold. The apostles become the new prophets of the Kingdom, casting out demons and raising people from the dead. Paul still speaks to us today in his articulate and astonishingly contemporary letters.

Besides the prophets, God seemed to delight in using common, ordinary—even unlikely—people: Rahab of Jericho, Ruth the Moabitess, even Cyrus the Gentile king of Babylon. Through whom does God speak today, in 1994? Or does God speak through people today?

God does. Sometimes he even speaks through children.

A Very Young Prophet

We have three children: two girls and one boy. While the kids were growing up our family life was a treasure I shall not forget. We were forever learning from as well as entertaining one another. God has at various times used each of our children to communicate powerful lessons to us.

For now I want to tell you about a time when Jonathan, our youngest, was seven. At that time, Karon and I were lay people at East Side Church of God. Mimi, our eldest, was entering the seventh grade, and we had signed up to be parents of the month for the youth group. This meant that it was our dubious privilege to provide food for the thundering horde on specific occasions. The first of these was the "Back to School Bash" in September. The whole family went along. At Mimi's insistent urging, Jodi and Jonathan promised to busy themselves out of the way. Several parents brought food for the hundred plus crowd that turned out. We took a crock pot of Sloppy Joe mix and packages of buns. Others brought soft drinks, potato chips, and paper plates, napkins, and cups.

We arrived early, and were set up and ready when the kids arrived, a herd of stampeding buffaloes. They thundered into the room with a noise not unlike an approaching tornado. When they dispersed they left a trail of ice chunks, empty two-liter bottles, and crushed potato chips. In the room next door they were to be entertained by Ken Long, now senior pastor at Vero Beach First Church of God, then a seminary student. Ken is loaded with talent. That night he played a banjo, guitar, and fiddle. Probably more. He sang some crazy songs and before long, even the new seventh graders were involved. Knowing how Jonathan loved music, I ran off to find him, and brought him back to the outside hallway. There I issued my stern fatherly instructions. This was a high and holy privilege, not to be repeated if he didn't exhibit his very best behavior. No talking. No moving. To reinforce the message, I then ran my right index finger under my chin as though slitting my throat, and made a hissing sound. He nodded solemnly. His antenna had received my transmission. We sneaked into the room full of teenagers, and Jonathan sat against the back wall. I moved a little way off to find some floor space, and was quickly absorbed in a story Ken was telling about a young teenager's conversion.

In five or ten minutes I felt a small hand against my elbow. I looked down into the wide green eyes of my seven-year-old son. When my eyes met his, he whispered, "Dad, isn't it great?"

"Jon!" I mouthed silently. "What are you doing here?" I repeated the slicing of the throat sign along with a menacing hissing sound under my breath. Jon withdrew, temporarily subdued.

Not more than a few minutes later Jon returned. The little hand again grasped my elbow. This is too much! I thought to myself, getting ready to grab the offending child, whisk him out into the hallway, and reinforce my threats with some understandable physical activity. The moment I caught his gaze, my heart stopped. I instantly was eight years of age at the old tabernacle at Whitehall Camp in western Pennsylvania. I could suddenly hear my Dad preaching, especially the closing illustration about John Huss being burned at the stake for his faith in Jesus Christ. I could feel my heart swelling as though it would break and remembered the hot tears spilling down my cheeks. I could hear my mother as she leaned over to ask if I was okay, and again heard the only response I knew how to make. "I think I'm sick."

Jon's eyes still stared up at me. He repeated his earlier phrase. "Dad, isn't it great?"

"Jon, would you like to go and pray?"

He nodded, dumbly, his eyes reflecting the call his soul was hearing.

We went into the eating room where discarded paper plates overflowed wastebaskets. I found a metal folding chair and the two of us knelt there for a moment, ready to pray. God interrupted me, basically suggesting that he was handling this now, and I was not needed. I quickly gave Jon a couple of instructions. Listen for God's voice. When you hear it, pay attention.

I turned to look at him as I left the room. He looked so small,

15

kneeling at that folding chair all by himself in the middle of an empty room.

Some time later when the program was over, Jodi came inquiring after Jon. "I can't find him," she declared. "Well," I offered, glancing around the room haphazardly, "he was here a few minutes ago. See if you can find him."

Fifteen minutes later Jodi arrived, with Jon in tow. "Something's wrong with Jon," she announced, "Just look at him!"

His face was puffy from crying and tears streaked his cheeks. His eyes were red. When he tried to speak, he burst into fits of sobbing. Both of the girls offered their opinions about what could have caused such crying. Karon and I only looked at each other and wondered. All the way home the girls kept after Jon. What happened? Why are you crying? Did someone hurt you? Jon shook his head once in a while, but mostly sat there sniffling, unable to find a voice.

At bedtime that night we gathered as usual for prayer. We rotated each night to one of the children's three beds. Tonight we knelt by Jon's bed. Jodi, the practical one, probed again for some kind of explanation, "Jon," she reasoned, "This is the pits! Can't you tell us what happened to you?"

We waited quietly for a few minutes while Jon struggled to gain composure. All these hours after his experience he was still visibly moved. He finally found his voice. Softly and clearly he said the words I will never forget. "God was so close, I couldn't speak."

Later that night I lay awake in bed long after Karon had fallen asleep. All I could remember was the story of Samuel, the young lad dedicated to God. As a boy he moved to live in the tabernacle with the priest, Eli. Over and over I relived in my mind how, when little Samuel heard God's voice, he must have stumbled into Eli's room, thinking it was Eli's voice he had heard, never dreaming God himself was nearby. I thought about how Eli must have pondered Samuel's repeated visits, and how he with effort recalled how, years before, he himself had heard God's voice. But, the story goes, Eli was far from God. His own sons were an abomination to God, seducing young women in the courts of the Lord and stealing the meat of sacrifice for their own tables. As I lay in the dark one sentence from the scriptural narrative suddenly stood out in my

16

mind as though in neon lights: "The word of the Lord was rare in those days."

Now God was asking me a question, "Why was it rare, Dave?" I immediately knew why. No one was listening. The adults weren't listening. The priest's sons weren't listening. Even Eli wasn't listening. So God spoke to a little child, barely old enough to attend elementary school.

Again I remembered Jon's face as he said, "God was so close, I couldn't speak." How long has it been, I thought, that I sensed God's presence like that? Too long. I was so very busy about the Lord's work, but I was too busy to be with the Lord. My spiritual life was gradually drifting. My personal devotions had long since gone by the wayside.

Now with tears, I pleaded in the darkness. "God, I want an experience like that! I want you to be so close to me that I can't speak. I want you, God."

God's response was sobering but loving. He said, "Finally. At last you want me and not only what I give. Finally you hunger for what I alone can bring." That night revolutionized my life. And a little boy was the tool through whom God spoke.

GOD IS INTENSELY INTERESTED IN US

Lots of people today struggle to believe God has any interest in our world. Why? Here are some of the more obvious reasons.

1. Intellectualism ridicules it. Philosophers (and those in their college classes) struggle to prove or disprove the existence of God. When one discovers that the very existence of God cannot be maintained with intellectual integrity,[7] further discussion about any professed interest on the part of God seems pointless. Education itself often elevates human reasoning to the point that God is no longer a feasible part of our lives. It is my observation that less educated people tend to have deeper faith experiences than those with advanced degrees.

2. The cultural climate in North America increasingly embraces tolerance and diversity, and the Christian assertion of a personal God who saves some but not all persons leaves a bad taste in the mouths of many. The public is backing away from the

17

traditional stand of the church on issues such as abortion and homosexuality. The buffoonery of prominent Christians like Jimmy Swaggart and Jim and Tammy Faye Bakker only intensifies the scorn with which many view Christianity as a whole. Ultimately, God suffers from the bad press.

3. Disappointing personal experiences with God, especially prayers apparently unanswered, insulate even Christians, in time, from the comforting assurance that God really does care about us. Television constantly blasts us with bad news of violated children, distant warfare, and natural calamities. One begins to wonder how God could possibly be interested and permit such global devastation of innocence and beauty.

But we can know God is intensely interested in us. To believe in God at all takes faith. In other words, we choose to believe, even in the absence of scientific proof of human logic. But we don't have to park our brains at the curb to do so. Observe how God constantly takes the initiative.

Creation Proves God's Interest

Our planet was God's idea in the first place. Even if you hold the view that Genesis is not a literal accounting of days and events, you can acknowledge that God was the Prime Mover, the First Cause. And why would he move, or cause? Because God was interested, that's why.

God took the initiative to express his incredible diversity and creativity: he made a staggering number of animal species, copious varieties of plant life, vast oceans and shimmering coral reefs teeming with fish, towering Himalayan mountains and windswept deserts.

God took the initiative to bestow the gifts of sight and sound, taste and touch on creatures of all sizes. The pesky housefly with its maddeningly quick reflexes and remarkable vision is a whole world of diversity within itself. Dolphins are fun-loving and compassionate, apparently communicating in their own language and caring for the young and sick among their number. Gorillas have been taught hundreds of human words and are able to convey abstract concepts.

God took the initiative to create humankind, the crown of God's creation. Not only are we set apart by the marvelous complexity of our bodies and minds, but we have been made in God's image.[8] Inborn in every people of the world lies the transcendent belief that there is more to life than just seventy years. Something eternal lives within the human personality. It was God's initiative to create us so.

No sooner had man and woman been created than God took the initiative to develop a relationship with them. The writer of Genesis says that he walked with them in the cool of the day.[9] Certainly God does not "need" human companionship, or anything else for that matter. Yet human beings somehow satisfy a place in God's heart that no other part of creation can fill. How else can you explain the persistent, consistent program of the Creator to build relationships with people?

God Chooses a People Because He Is Interested

"The Lord said to Abram, 'Leave your country, your people and your father's household and go to the land I will show you.

'I will make you into a great nation
and I will bless you;
I will make your name great,
and you will be a blessing.
I will bless those who bless you,
and whoever curses you I will curse;
and all people on earth
will be blessed through you.' "[10]

So begins the Covenant, the solemn binding of God to men and men to God. Who thought it up? Who designed it? Who wanted it? Who initiated it? God did. Incredibly, painstakingly, patiently—so patient as to surpass human comprehension—God ties himself to this imperfect man and his family through the years. When Isaac, the miracle child, had grown into a strapping lad and became the center of his ancient father's world, God tests the relationship and finds it true. What is going on here?

It's a love story of a God who's hopelessly in love with his creation. It's the account of a God who is crazy for us, so crazy that for hundreds of years he pursues these people, these Hebrews born of Abraham's line. He sends Joseph on ahead so they will be preserved in times of famine. He raises up a leader in Pharaoh's court who will ultimately rescue them from that very power. He pampers them with quail and manna in the wilderness. He leads them to the land promised centuries earlier and then helps them conquer it. He gives them the king they cry for against his better judgment, and then sends prophets when the kings lose their focus. He follows them into captivity brought on by their own selfishness and idolatry, then rescues them again and brings them home.

In Hosea one catches a glimpse of the lengths to which God intends to go. Was there ever so endearing a tale as this one? Hosea (the God figure) marries a prostitute (the chosen people) he knows by nature and habit is unfaithful. Is it not God who pursues her when she has left Hosea with the children? Does not God buy her back, and then stand embracing her, wiping the tears from her eyes, telling her,

> I will show my love to the one I called "Not my loved one."
> I will say to those called "Not my people."
> > "You are my people";
> > and they will say, "You are my God."?[11]

God Sent a Savior Because He Is Interested

A young preacher named Ezekiel was born after the remnant of the Israelite nation was taken into captivity in Babylon. The memories of the great Exodus were practically erased by the pain of the present. The stories of Joshua and Jericho were mostly forgotten. The glory of King David's reign was a bitter memory, for the great temple built by Solomon was now destroyed, Jerusalem was burned, and few were left who could personally remember anything good that had come from the hand of the Lord.

Perhaps Ezekiel was sitting late one night, gazing at the stars as they twinkled overhead. "Dear God, the Babylonians are like these stars—numberless. And what is left of us, the so-called 'Chosen people?' " A gentle breeze began to ruffle Ezekiel's hair. It was a genesis wind, fragrant with the energy of creation. It was born from the heart of God, our same God who takes the initiative not once, not twice, but over and over and over again. The heavenly wind stirred more than Ezekiel's hair. It penetrated his mind and heart and finally stirred in his soul. Visions now came, fantastic visions of God on the throne, of valleys of dead men, and of destruction.[12] But there were also wonderful visions: visions of God's Word bringing a dead army back to life, visions of hope, and visions of the kingdom of God.

In the last several chapters of Ezekiel,[13] he is describing one such vision. He sees the new Jerusalem, or the kingdom of God. From a resplendent and majestic temple flows a marvelous, life-giving river. Life springs forth profusely everywhere its waters stream. Even the Dead Sea is restored by the this wondrous river, which turns brine into sparkling water where fish dart and fruit trees endlessly blossom.

In a growing crescendo, Ezekiel describes the city, its measurements and gates. Finally comes this climactic verse, "And the name of the city from that time on will be:
THE LORD IS THERE."[14]

What's Going on Here?

Ezekiel saw cleanly right into the heart of God: God longs to be with his people. This has always been God's dream, from the beginning of time. The city of God is still bright in God's mind, a place where sin no longer howls, where idolatry at last is mute. Ezekiel saw the future when God himself would come to earth, wrapped in human skin. Ezekiel saw the city which the Savior would build. Even this visionary man hardly grasped how gloriously his words would be fulfilled in the coming of God himself to live among his unlikely treasures. Matthew tells us, "All this took place to fulfill what the Lord had said through the prophet: 'The virgin will be with child and will give birth to a son, and they will call him Immanuel'—which means, 'God with us.' "[15] The echo of Ezekiel's description reverberates in our ears. "And the name of the city … will be: 'THE LORD IS THERE.' "

An Interested Savior Takes the Initiative

Hebrews tells us that Jesus is the exact representation of God's being. The more we study Jesus' life, the more we will understand God's character.

Jesus' entire ministry was spent taking the initiative. That certainly reflects the God of the Old Testament, doesn't it? In the New Testament, we follow Jesus from Galilee to Jerusalem to Samaria. He called the fishermen to be disciples. Initiative. He sat down and taught like a scribe. Initiative. He confronted Pharisees and anyone else who needed confronting. Initiative.

One of my favorite stories illustrates Christ's compassionate nature as well as his bent toward taking the initiative We read in Mark 6:45–52 that, after the feeding of the five thousand, Jesus "made his disciples get into the boat and go on ahead of him to Bethsaida, while he dismissed the crowd. After leaving them, he went into the hills to pray.

"When evening came, the boat was in the middle of the lake, and he was alone on land. He saw the disciples straining at the oars, because the wind was against them. About the fourth watch of the night he went out to them, walking on the lake."

The miracle of walking on water usually takes center stage in this narrative. For the moment, however, note that although Jesus was praying in the hills, he had one eye on the disciples in the boat. They were seasoned seamen, fully capable of handling things on their own. Yet "he saw" them and "went out to them." Since he had no boat, he got there the best way he could. Don't be distracted in the manner by which he went, and lose the point that he saw and he went. Why? Because he was intensely interested in them, he took the initiative.

An Interested God Sends the Holy Spirit

One last example of God's initiative comes at the end of Christ's earthly sojourn. The trials and the horrible crucifixion were over. The glorious resurrection was fact. The risen Christ had appeared several times to the disciples. Now came the ascension and that moment for which the church had been (unknowingly) waiting: the coming to earth of the Holy Spirit of God.

In John 14:18 Jesus had promised that "I will not leave you as orphans; I will come to you." He later explains about the coming of the Holy Spirit,[16] and in the subsequent chapters of John, describes his work and distinguishing characteristics.

In Acts 2 God does send the Holy Spirit with the noise of a thunderous windstorm, which just happens to attract an attentive crowd on whom the newly spirit-filled apostles can practice. Energized and anointed, a transformed Peter finds that he is finally able to do the things Jesus had said, and there's no stopping him any more. God planned it and initiated it. What will he initiate with you?

OBVIOUSLY, THE CREATOR OF THE UNIVERSE WANTS TO COMMUNICATE WITH US.

A God who speaks through every possible means, who takes the initiative to establish relationships with us that will transform our lives, who sends not only a Savior but the Holy Spirit, what is God telling us?

You Are Important to Me

God came in person. What does it mean to go in person? It means that the one to whom you go is important to you.

The business world is more than ever aware of the value of the personal touch. Scores of new books hammer away at their professional audiences that without personable, competent, friendly people in customer relations, their business will simply not survive. The new gospel at McDonalds and IBM is the gospel of personal contact. Nothing says, "I care," so much as a personal visit, a handwritten note, or a telephone call—from the executive, not the secretary.

Wall Street gurus are learning what Christians have known all along (although often we have been poor at putting it into practice): when you care enough, you go. Church growth statistics constantly support this fact: congregations who are growing are touching people personally. They're visiting them, helping them fit into support groups, and caring for their spiritual needs.

I had a friend once who couldn't stand weddings. Besides that, he rarely ever attended a wedding, even though it might be the marriage of one of his good friend's children. He saw them as occasions to flaunt wealth and make a social statement. Although my friend is a sensitive, caring person, he couldn't seem to understand why the friends whose weddings he did not attend were hurt and distant. But Jesus knew the importance of the personal touch. If it's important to those you love, it will be important to you. If you love them, you will go. Period.

Jesus came in person. Nothing demonstrates love and care more than this.

God is speaking through the incarnation, and he's saying, "You are important to me. I cared enough to come myself."

You Can Change the World

He sends *us* in person, too. God entrusts the greatest story ever told to you and me, to share with our faltering words and forgetful minds. "But we have this treasure in jars of clay to show that this all-surpassing power is from God and not from us."[17] Personal communication is irreplaceable. Mass saturation mailings are good for a beginning, but, as we learn from Jesus, nothing can replace the personal touch.

QUESTIONS FOR DISCUSSION

1. Describe someone you know whose life indicates he or she is "desperate to hear from God."

2. Have you ever heard God speak? Or do you know of someone who claims God has spoken to them? What were the circumstances?

3. Do you believe the age of miracles has passed? What reasons can you give?

4. Does God speak through people today? Has God used anyone to speak to you?

5. How can a Christian get beyond disappointing experiences in life when it seems prayers were unanswered?

6. What message to you from God is your favorite? How did it happen?

NOTES

1. This story appears beginning on page 14.
2. Hebrews 1:1–3
3. Psalm 8:3, 4; Psalm 104:3
4. Psalms 104:1–4
5. Job 38:1ff
6. From one of Gerald Marvel's sermons as recalled by Richard Willowby.
7. That is, human reasoning, even at its finest, admits the existence or nonexistence of God is beyond scientific proof.

8. Genesis 1:26
9. Genesis 3:8
10. Genesis 12:1–3
11. Hosea 2:23
12. See chapter 2 for a discussion of the vision of the Valley of Dry Bones (Ezekiel 37).
13. Ezekiel 47–49
14. Ezekiel 48:35, italics added
15. Matthew 1:22–23
16. John 14:26ff
17. 2 Corinthians 4:7

2

God Is Speaking through His Word

Hebrews 4:12–13

It is common for us to categorize certain objects as old.

1. A man with a cane shuffles through the mall. He walks with effort. His face is wrinkled, a crumpled leaf. He's definitely old.
2. A song from the 1940s plays on the radio. An unusual beat sways gently and there are no electric guitars. Our teenagers classify this as "ancient music."
3. *National Geographic* carries an article about an archaeological find in Africa. A newly discovered skeleton is radio-carbon dated more than a hundred thousand years. Old!
4. Halley's comet returns, an infrequent visitor from the outer reaches of space. No one knows how many millennia it has pursued its solitary path through the void. Absolutely old!

For minds such as ours, inclined to classify an object that has been around a mere sixty or seventy years as "old," the sweep of time inhabited by God is incomprehensible. A child recently confided in me that he planned to live to be at least 110 years old. Some time ago a gentleman in Georgia claimed to be 130. Abraham lived to be 185. Methuselah lasted 969 years. Old? Not more than a few fragments in the universe. We are rather like mayflies that spring to life, mate, and die within five hours.

Once in a while our tiny brains are penetrated with the true vastness of eternity. The first verses of John's gospel are arrows of light shot into our dim hearts: "In the beginning was the Word, and the Word was with God, and the Word was God. He was with God in the beginning."[1] These words stir the centuries and millennia. God has not only lived for million, billions, or perhaps trillions of years. God has always lived.

Not only God the Father has always lived. His Son, Jesus Christ, also has existed forever. Long before he lay as a baby in Bethlehem, God's Son waded the deep recesses of the universe, molding stars and masterminding moonbeams. John tells us "through him all things were made; without him nothing was made that has been made. In him was life, and that life was the light of men."[2]

The writer of Hebrews picks up this thought and expands it even further. "The Son is the radiance of God's glory and the exact representation of his being, sustaining all things by his powerful word."[3] In other words, Jesus expresses what is on God's mind. Jesus is not just the translator for God, he actually embodies and expresses God's boundless power. John says, he is the Word of God, the Word that became flesh and walked among us.[4]

These marvelous and lofty concepts do not translate easily into the shallow level on which many of us live from day to day. Our brains are glutted with FAX transmissions, computer programs, bank accounts, and sports events. Church life sags into uninspiring routines filled with printed orders of worship and scripture readings. The Bible becomes just another reference book from which we select texts for sermons or verses to support what we believe. Slowly, imperceptibly, we lose sight of the eternal Word and muddle along with a word or two.

But the Bible is not just another book. It is not even another holy book. "The word of God is living and active. Sharper than any double-edged sword, it penetrates even to dividing soul and spirit, joints and marrow; it judges the thoughts and attitudes of the heart. Nothing in all creation is hidden from God's sight. Everything is uncovered and laid bare before the eyes of him to whom we must give account."[5]

The Bible you carry is not itself eternal in the sense that the paper, ink, and cover will last forever. However, the truth within its pages is in-breathed by the Son of God. That same breath of God ruffled the Genesis deeps to sprout a world,[6] filled Ezekiel's vision with dead men come to life,[7] and gusted into Jerusalem on the Day of Pentecost to give birth to the church.[8] The Word of God (God's Son), creator of all life, inspired the written word that we know as the Bible. Therein lies the key to unlock humankind's destiny and the road map for life's journey.

Since whole libraries are filled with the studies of God's word, and since its truth can never be exhausted, let me, for this small chapter, take you to a high hill that offers a panoramic perspective of God's fantastic message.

The first great view from God's Word is this ...

NO SITUATION IS TOO HOPELESS FOR GOD

If anyone knew this the people of Israel should have known it.

There was Abraham, the father of the race, and his wife, Sarah. These two ancients were far beyond child-bearing years when God promised that he would send them a child of their own. It seemed hopeless!

They couldn't believe that Sarah, with one foot in the grave, would ever have her other foot in the maternity ward. But God anointed that withered womb, and Isaac was born to a woman in her nineties. That makes the headlines of even the *National Enquirer* seem tame in comparison. Nothing is too hopeless for God!

There was that whole series of miracles that hammered Pharaoh into submission forcing him to free the Israelites. Perhaps the most climactic was when the entire nation was hemmed in by the Red Sea on one hand and Pharaoh's armies were galloping toward them on the only path of retreat. What to do? Drown? Commit mass suicide? It seemed hopeless! They couldn't imagine that Pharaoh or the Red Sea could be moved.

But God blasted open a path of escape created right through the ocean depths. The Israelites went free while Pharaoh's armies searched for life vests. Nothing is too hopeless for God!

29

There was that great fortified city of Jericho, rising up before them like granite cliffs; inaccessible, unyielding, and massive. How like ants they must have felt, surveying the soldiers of Jericho strutting high above them on the ramparts. God said, "Take the city!" It seemed hopeless! They couldn't imagine how even God could devise a way to breach the walls.

But God had a plan, and used a weapon every baby is able to use the moment he announced his entry into the world: the human voice. The walls collapsed in ruin and the city was conquered. Nothing is too hopeless for God!

God Gives a Vision

Ezekiel[9] was a Jew living in exile in Babylon. When he first saw the light of day, Abraham, Moses, and Joshua had long since died. These stories of God's great power seemed like fairy tales. Now the people of Israel were in captivity. They had been taken as slaves to foreign countries. The greatness of Jerusalem was a memory. The great kings of David and Solomon were buried and gone. The bravery of Israel's armies marching under the banner of a powerful and invincible God seemed almost too much to believe.

While a few of the faithful still talked about the glory of Israel, the great majority had given up, saying things like, "Those days are over and done with. God is through with us. We will never again see his hand at work in our midst. We are condemned to live as foreigners in a foreign land."

"Our hope is gone!" they would surely cry, "God may have saved our people from captivity once, but he won't do it again. Our future is desolate. Israel is finished as a nation, and God is silent."

God, contrary to his critics' opinions, was not through. He called Ezekiel into the ministry, advising him that, "The people to whom I am sending you are obstinate and stubborn. Say to them, 'This is what the Sovereign Lord says.' "[10]

Were Ezekiel like us, he probably had a difficult time imagining just how God was going to do anything with his compatriots. "What can he do?" he must have mused. "How can even God change obstinate and stubborn hearts? How can even God open hearts that will not listen?"

God illustrated for this preacher who was down on his optimism just what he had in mind. Ezekiel, guided by the hand of the Lord, found himself on a supernatural trip. God plunked him down in a valley filled with bones. It was a human junkyard, the valley floor covered with bones like piles of driftwood after a storm. Back and forth Ezekiel was taken, mile after mile. Skulls, vertebrae, femurs, and ribs littered his pathway. Clambering over clavicles, he finally found a small path of ground relatively free from bones. Kicking a couple of phalanges out of the way, Ezekiel stopped. It seemed that God was reading his mind.

"Zeke?"

"Yes, Sir!"

"Can these bones live?"

It was quite a question. Ezekiel had already seen enough bones to last a lifetime. Obviously, these were not bones from the recently dead. They had been here for years, maybe decades. Ezekiel may have thought to himself something like we would have thought, Pretty gruesome, Lord. Pretty hopeless.

Ezekiel sensed that God was testing his faith. The last few months came flooding into his mind: the doubts about God's power, the doubts about whether or not God was still active, the doubts about whether God had really been as stunning as the legendary tales claimed. But he also knew God had called him. God had singled him out. God was at work, in his life at least. Finally, he gave a diplomatic answer.

"O Sovereign Lord, you alone know."

"Okay, Zeke," God challenged, "preach your best sermon to this congregation, here. Tell them to sit up and take note of the kind of God you serve. Tell them they're going to come to life once more, and live, and breathe, have children, and raise families. I will do it, Zeke. I'm waiting to do it. I'm wanting to do it. I'm willing to do it. You preach the Word, Zeke. I'll do the work."

Ezekiel stood in that desolate place where life had once flourished. The wind moaned through the remains of a nation. Could God actually do what he said? It's bad enough to preach to a congregation that's half asleep. This group was deader than a doornail. Zeke hesitated momentarily. Suddenly there swept over him the compelling realization that he was not responsible for the results, but only for proclaiming God's word. And the power of that word filled his soul and spilled forth.

"Hey, you bones, you dry old bones. God is going to revolutionize you. The Sovereign Lord says he's going to bring you to life. The God who called Abraham and made a great nation from that old man is moving upon you. The God who stopped Pharaoh's armies cold is going to make an army out of you. The God who flattened Jericho's walls is here today, and he says, 'Live!' "

As Zeke preached his heart out a fresh breeze—a creation wind—began to blow through that deserted place. It was filled with freshness and fragrant with new life. The dry, lifeless wind of the desert became the singing of the Spirit of God, bathing death with life, flooding that desolate valley with energy and hope.

Ezekiel writes that, halfway through the sermon, the bones started to rattle and move. They joined themselves together. Tendons and ligaments formed at the joints. Nerves grew through vertebrae. Muscles glistened and newly formed skin covered arms and legs, faces and backs.

When he stopped preaching to gaze in wonder, God spoke. "Zeke, don't stop now. The Word of the Lord will make these bones not only bodies, but spirits. Preach, man, preach!"

"O great host," Zeke faltered, not quite sure how to address a thousand or so almost alive people. "God isn't finished with you, yet. He wants you to get up and move. You're going to walk. The great God of all the ages is working in this place, and his word to you today is to live, breathe, and stand up!"

Like a great congregation, the vast number of persons stood alive, ready, prepared to serve the Lord. An hour before there was death. Now life throbbed everywhere. The desolate silence of a graveyard now resonated with the sounds of life.

But Was It Real?

You may say, "This never really happened. Opening the Red Sea is one thing—that was historical. But this was only a vision. There never really was a geographical place called the Valley of Dry Bones."

True, it was not a geographical place. But it was nonetheless real. It was a spiritual place, the heart-home where the nation of Israel was living, clogged with the dry bones of broken dreams and devastated by unbelief and sin. The air was stale and heavy with bitterness and disillusionment. It is a place where millions live today, peopled by those who have given up on God and turned away from their source of life. The song they are moaning bears a tragic familiarity to that wailed by Ezekiel's contemporaries: "Our hope is gone and our future is hopeless."

The good news is that the Valley of Dry Bones became a place of spiritual renewal. Such renewal is always born first in the heart before it can transform the body. It is real because it is the salvation story, always fresh, always new. It is real because one day in your life and mine the Holy Spirit blew that same genesis wind into our hearts, transforming the hopeless remains of a sinful life into a person of incredible value and beauty. It is the story of the church, an army of living, breathing, spiritually alive people created from the discarded remnants of the damned.

God used this fantastic hyperbole of vision to impress upon Ezekiel—and us—that his power is limitless, awesome, and fantastic. God not only has a plan, but the power to make it come true. This was not just a five-year-old cured of the sniffles. This was not only a tubercular grandmother breathing freely once more. This was not a still-warm corpse that somebody could always say had not really died before God "brought it back to life." This was hopeless, friends. Not one person, or two people, but a nation. And God's power brought all of them back to life!

The Proof of God's Power

The irrefutable proof of this, of course, is the resurrection of Christ. Paul nails this down in Romans 15:17, 19 when he says, "And if Christ has not been raised, your faith is futile; you are still in your sins…. If only for this life we have hope in Christ, we are to be pitied more than all men."

When Jesus arrived in Bethany four days after Lazarus had been buried, he was confronted with two distraught sisters who berated and pleaded with him for not coming sooner. We can identify with their reaction, since there seemed to be no valid reason for Jesus' delay to their urgent summons when Lazarus lay dying. Jesus responded "Did I not tell you that if you believed, you would see the glory of God?"[11] His answer echoes Isaiah's words and hovers in our minds like angelic music, " 'For my thoughts are not your thoughts, neither are your ways my ways,' declares the Lord. 'As the heavens are higher than the earth, so are my ways higher than your ways and my thoughts than your thoughts.' "[12]

Mary and Martha could only guess at the fantastic events to which Jesus referred when he said, "I am the resurrection and the life. He who believes in me will live, even though he dies."[13]

This wonderful theme is repeated and magnified a few weeks later on Easter morning when the tear-blinded women gazed in shock at angels sitting where they expected to see a corpse. "Why do you look for the living among the dead? He is not here; he has risen! Remember how he told you, while he was still with you in Galilee: 'The Son of Man must be delivered into the hands of sinful men, be crucified, and on the third day be raised again.' "[14]

Why Is No Situation Too Hopeless for God?

God's Word pulses with the news that Something is going on in this world. Someone started it, and Someone intends to keep at it. In the face of devastating circumstance, discouraging events, and a personal devil, God's greater plan moves ahead to the glorious culmination of history. How else could Paul declare, "We are hard pressed on every side, but not crushed; perplexed but not in despair; persecuted but not forsaken; cast down, but not destroyed."[15]

The second great view ...

GOD HAS A PLAN

God's plan from the beginning has been to penetrate the void with life, to substitute light for darkness, life for death, purity for sinfulness, and love for hatred. We see it in the irrepressible urge to reproduce in the animal and plant world. We see it in the built-in capacity of nature to heal the environment from natural disasters like volcanoes and forest fires. Anyone contemplating seeds, for example, can only wonder at their incredible ingenuity and variety.

The Irresistible Spunk of Life

I am an amateur gardener. Growing flowers is one of my hobbies. The problems with any kind of gardening are basically three: bad soil, prolific weeds, and voracious bugs. One summer, I set aside a Saturday to weed my flower beds. My usual pattern was to start at one end and slowly (and with back-breaking effort) work my way around the yard. This particular day began with clear skies, temperate breezes, and brilliant sunshine. Birds sang, a hummingbird hovered in the nearby trellis, and all was well with the world. As the day wore on, my spirits sank in reverse proportion to the increase of annoying pain in my lower back. Grimly pushing ahead, I determined to complete the job to the corner before lunch. That was before I noticed that the section of flower beds standing between me and my lunch time goal were jubilant with a miniature clover of some kind that rejoices and flourishes even in cement-like soil, and which produces thousands of hair-fine roots which are practically impossible to dislodge. Time for lunch, now!

Modestly refreshed by a sandwich, iced tea, and a thirty-minute nap, I picked up my trusty trowel. Those weeds couldn't be that bad! I trotted out to the flower bed, ignored the complaints of my back and knees, and squatted over the offending clover. I was immediately startled by what felt like little grains of sand being flung against my face. What I discovered in the next few moments was that, whenever I stepped on the compact weed where mature flowers had gone to seed, the crushing of the weed by my foot or trowel activated hundreds of tiny, spring-loaded seed pods, so tiny they were invisible to the naked eye. Totally absorbed by this amazing phenomenon, I went from weed to weed, banging them with my trowel to set off the little catapult seed pods, listening to the tiny pattering of the seeds against nearby foliage, and marveling at God's ingenuity. Later it dawned on me: I had just reseeded the whole flower bed with that annoying weed! I felt the experiment well worth it. In fact, when Karon came home, I took her out to the pesky clover to enjoy some seed catapulting before dinner.

After the devastating firestorms that swept through Yellowstone National Park several years ago, naturalists assured us that in many respects, such seeming tragedy was in fact a blessing. As a matter of fact, the lodge pole pine cannot reproduce without forest fires, for their pine cones only open under the fires' extreme heat. Over and over throughout nature we find similar illustrations of its inborn resilience, planned carefully by God.

God's Plan to Create a Family

We should not be surprised at the irresistible resilience of nature to survive and reproduce. This same deliberate determination shows up from Genesis to Revelation as God moves to create a family for himself. God's disappointment is almost palpable in the Garden of Eden when Adam and Eve fall prey to the Enemy. Through the centuries God relentlessly searches for individuals who are sensitive to his love and open to his leading and concerns. The prophet who wrote, "I will put my law in their minds and write it on their hearts"[16] likely could not even dream that God's love would compel him to come himself and live among us as a human being. And who could imagine the horror and wonder of the atonement?

In chapter one we mentioned how Abraham heard God's voice and ventured forth, blazing the faith trail for all of us. Unfortunately for many of us, the following words are so familiar they have lost their ability to startle us: "I will make you into a great nation and I will bless you."[17] We must not lose sight of the amazing drive from God's heart that compels him to seek intimate friends among the human race.

The global scope of God's plan, glimpsed sporadically in the Old Testament, comes clearly into focus in the New Testament. Jesus explains, "For God did not send his Son into the world to condemn the world, but to *save the world through Him.*"[18]

God will neither be put off nor discouraged by the continuous defection of his people. God's directions to Ezekiel contain these words, "*they* say, 'Our bones are dried up and our hope is gone; we are cut off.' [But] *the Sovereign Lord* says, 'I will bring you back.... I will put my Spirit in you and you will live.... Then you will know that I the Lord have spoken, and I have done it, declares the Lord.' "[19]

God Has the Power to Carry Out This Plan

Many sweeping and grandiose schemes have failed for financing or resources. Legend tells of a mighty and powerful king whose kingdom expanded under his wise rule and beneficent government. In time he began to believe he really was more than just a king, that his great kingdom was divinely ordained, that a touch of divinity crowned his authority.

As the years went by, it became apparent that he was losing touch with reality, for he attempted more and more bizarre demonstrations of a supposed divine power his people knew was not there.

In one of his last official acts, he commanded his servants to take his throne to the beach, and to carry him, seated thereon, to the very edge of the surf when the tide was out. Here he would prove that even the forces of nature were at his command.

He read a royal pronouncement decreeing that the tides must stop. And he actually believed they would. As his embarrassed people watched, they saw the truth of this ancient saying, "Time and tide wait for no man." The waves advanced and washed over his shoes. Soon they were splashing against his legs. Time and again his servants moved this throne up the beach, only to be assaulted again by the relentless waves that were no respecter of persons and were not stopped by a man's decree—even though that man be a mighty king with great influence and power.

We do not hear of this king again. No doubt his rule soon ended in disgrace and we hope a humbler and wiser man ascended to the throne.

God's Power Is His Word

Jesus, unlike the king of legend, is divine, the living Word of God. It was about Jesus, God's Word, that John writes, "That which was from the beginning, which we have heard, which we have seen with our eyes, which we have looked at, and our hands have touched—this we proclaim concerning the Word of life. The life appeared; we have seen it and testify to it, and we proclaim to you the eternal life, which was with the Father and has appeared to us."[20]

Jesus' words, unlike those of the king of legend, are all powerful. Jesus commanded, "Be still" and the weather obeyed.[21] Jesus called to Lazarus, dead and buried four days earlier, and Lazarus walked out of the tomb and was reunited with his incredulous sisters.[22] It was Jesus' voice that called order out of chaos, for "he is the image of the invisible God, the firstborn over all creation. For by him all things were created: things in heaven and on earth, visible and invisible, whether thrones or powers or rulers or authorities; all things were created by him and for him. He is before all things, and in him all things hold together."[23]

Jesus, unlike the king of legend, is eternal, for "the Word of the Lord stands forever."[24] Unlike the words of humankind, God's Word sees beyond the physical realm to lay bare the secrets of the heart.[25] One cannot separate the power of God from the Word of God. It is inexorable, infinite, and marvelously dependable.

As the rain and the snow
    come down from heaven,
    and do not return to it
    without watering the earth
    and making it bud and flourish
    … so is my word that goes out from my mouth:
It will not return to me empty,
    but will accomplish what I desire
    and achieve the purpose for which I sent it.[26]

The third great view ...

GOD'S STRATEGY FOR CHANGING HOPELESS SITUATIONS

It is a terrific encouragement to realize that God initiates change where hopelessness abounds. When we are too discouraged even to pray, God is working, taking advantage of seemingly inconsequential events to tune our ears to his voice.

God Takes You to a Valley

God's Reality Therapy

In college psychology, one is taught about a great variety of therapies for those who need counseling. Of course, they're all intended to bring the individual back to emotional and psychological health. Separated by many years from my undergraduate days, I remember very few of those schools of thought. It seemed that every new psychology professor of any stature introduced yet another means of plumbing the depths of the human psyche. For example, Rogerian therapy advocated a "nondirective" emphasis. Such counselors mirror the thoughts of their counselees, repeating their thoughts back to them in hopes that they already have the answer inside, but just cannot discern it.

Perhaps it's my strict, conservative upbringing, but I always thought "reality" therapy made the most sense. Such therapy advocates that the counselor respond to the patient as might a good friend, pulling no punches. This approach is finding increasing support from many quarters. For example, the intervention and confrontation techniques utilized by counselors of alcoholics and their families advocates telling it like it is.

Long before psychological or scientific terms were coined, God called Ezekiel and took him to a valley of dry bones. You might say that God is a reality therapist. As you read the account, note that God first asked Ezekiel to walk back and forth. It was then that Ezekiel observed that the bones in the valley were very, very dry.

God didn't cover up the problems caused by sin and idolatry.

Rather, he helped Ezekiel finally understand (a) their horrible effect, and then (b) how miraculously God's power could bring healing and hope.

God didn't say, "You don't have a problem." He said, "I will bring you back." God didn't say, "Think positively and you'll be okay." He said, "Sin and disbelief did this, but, I will open your graves."

Diagnosis is often the difference between healing and death. The genius of God's approach must not be overlooked. God gave Ezekiel spiritual discernment, not a fat bank account or $5 million in the lottery. As you read the Old Testament you will find that false prophets often foretold peace when, in fact, God said peace was impossible.

A woman who married poorly continuously observed that she was "bearing her cross." It was no cross. It was a foolish marriage. God does not rationalize. God redeems. Where is your valley of dry bones? God will take you there, if you are willing.

God Asks Questions

Once Ezekiel realized where he was, how many bones there were, and how long they'd been there, God asked him, "Can these bones live?" In other words, Can God change this? Is it possible? Do you believe? When we see our valley and the reasons for it, God will invariably ask, "Can these bones live?"

"Do you want to get well?"[27] he queried the man who had lain by the pool for thirty-eight years. It seems like a foolish question, but God wanted to know what that man thought about himself and his situation. Once God has taken you to your valley, God wants to know what you think about (a) your situation and (b) whether you will participate in the healing process.

God Asks You to Apply His Word

Ezekiel was instructed to do only one thing, to prophesy to the bones. By telling him to prophesy, God was specifically ordering one thing: apply God's Word to this specific event. Prophecy is the "speaking forth" of God's will. Prophets were not to share their own opinions, but only God's Word. Prophets were often unpopular. No doubt they were at times misunderstood. None of this changed the rules, however. God's view was not humanity's view, and only God's view could save the day.

When confronted by the valleys of life, God does not ask us to parrot human advice. God challenges us to apply the power of the resurrection. Paul understood this. "I keep asking that the God of our Lord Jesus Christ, the glorious Father, may give you the Spirit of wisdom and revelation, so that you may know him better. I pray also that the eyes of your heart may be enlightened in order that you may know the hope to which he has called you, the riches of his glorious inheritance in the saints, and his incomparably great power for us who believe. That power is like the working of his mighty strength, which he exerted in Christ when he raised him from the dead and seated him at his right hand in the heavenly realms."[28]

There is a time for human comfort. Jesus himself valued the companionship of his friends, and asked them to pray with him in his hour of temptation.[29] But no human thought can save from sin. No human word, though wise and eloquent, can raise from the dead and redeem the lost. It was not Ezekiel's words that transformed a valley of death into a host of living, breathing people. God did that.

"But what does it say? 'The word is near you; it is in your mouth and in your heart,' that is, the word of faith we are proclaiming. That if you confess with your mouth, 'Jesus is Lord,' and believe in your heart that God raised him from the dead, you will be saved. For it is with your heart that you believe and are justified, and it is with your mouth that you confess and are saved."[30]

What Happens When God's Word Is Applied

God's Word always brings resurrection. It may be the fantastic rebirth in Ezekiel's Valley of Dry Bones or the miraculous resurrection of Lazarus. It may be the remarkable experience of Saul, the "least of the apostles."[31]

Two hundred fifty years ago, a small boy in London named John dreamed of going to sea.[32] He frequented the harbor, watching the huge three-masted sailing vessels his father sailed. They came and went from all over the world, speaking to him of distant places, coral seas, palm trees, and exotic adventures. "One day," he would say to himself as he lay on the huge bales of outgoing cargo, "I will be the captain of a ship like these!"

John's mother was a deeply religious woman who lived all of her short life in poor health. She died when John was only a lad of six. Since his father was away at sea, John was boarded with neighbors until the day his father finally returned to find his house locked and hung with faded crepe. His father was a stern man who permitted no weeping, even for a mother or wife's death. He promptly remarried and John became an unloved stepson attending a private school with a tyrant of a headmaster who wielded a cane and birch rod.

His father, when at home during John's holidays, kept him in fear and bondage, breaking his spirit. John's formal education came to an abrupt halt on his eleventh birthday, his father taking his pre-adolescent son to sea on the first of five voyages that grounded him in seamanship and hardened his hatred toward his father.

John was pressed into service in the British navy beginning a career at sea that would last for many years. Life on board was incredibly brutal. Conscripted sailors like John were as horribly mistreated as slaves in the South. Seasickness swept over him for days at a time. His fierce temper and poor judgment earned him a public flogging that scarred him for life.

In time he mastered the difficult routine of working sailing vessels in those days before radio, radar, refrigeration, and sanitation. Years later he became a partner on a ship bound for the Ivory Coast of Africa. The slave trade was lucrative and John was ready to make a fortune. Lying off the coast they would trade goods with disreputable merchants who dealt in people's lives. While the ship lay at anchor for days and sometimes weeks, small rowboats would ferry back and forth, bringing Africans who had been sold into slavery. They would be taken below decks to lie in chains until they arrived at their new home in the colonies, now the United States. Shackled into spaces unfit for cattle or swine, unable to move even to relieve themselves, fully one-third of the slaves would die before reaching their new home. As John unchained the dead and threw them overboard, he secretly felt this was God's mercy, for he had heard tales of how slaves were treated on the cotton plantations in the colonies.

Still unable to control his fiery independence and rash judgments, John fell afoul of his partner, the ship's captain. In a nightmarish twist of fate, the shameful sea captain made John his personal slave, and had a blacksmith weld iron manacles around his ankles. Chained to the decks throughout driving rainstorms, starved nearly to death, he survived by sheer stubbornness and God's grace.

Two years passed. He was finally rescued from his living hell, a bitter and cruel man. Bearing the scars of a flogging during his navy days, brutalized by his many experiences in the slave trade, embittered by the reversal of fate that reduced him from fortune-hunter to serf on an African plantation, he lashed out with blasphemies so acid they shocked hard-bitten mariners. The captain by whose mercy he now voyaged to London often wished he had never set eyes on this sour and ungrateful man. Newton himself had little reason to live. Long ago he had forgotten the words learned at his mother's knee. Or so he thought.

"We are sinking!" Young Newton leaped from his bunk and without pausing to pull on thicker garments against the cold he rushed toward the companion hatch to give help on deck. The captain called down for a knife. As Newton ran back to fetch it, another of the ship's company dashed up the companion ladder and was swept overboard by a wave.

> Newton found the knife and came on deck. He judged at once, from his years of experience in the merchant marine and the navy, that the ship might sink at any moment. A wave had torn away the upper timbers so that she filled fast. The hull was weak after eighteen months in the tropics, and the Greyhound would have sunk already had she been carrying a slave trade cargo.
>
> The ship tossed and rolled. Newton struggled in the darkness to one of the pumps and joined another man pumping hard, while other bailed with buckets, or tore up clothes to help staunch the leaks. When day broke

and they found themselves still alive, Newton called out cheerfully above the wind as he pumped, "In a few days this distress will serve us to talk of, over a glass of wine!"

"No," said his mate. His tone was grave, "It's too late now." He was preparing to die.[33]

The storm battered the ship for days. Alone below decks, the horror of John's life rose before him like the waves that washed over what was left of his ship. Memories of panic-stricken slaves and crew members he had beaten for insubordination flooded upon his mind. He thought often of scriptures that came unbidden to his mind. But each one was dismissed. He was too wretched, too low, too despicable to be within reach of Jesus Christ. But one evening he ran across these verses in Luke 11:12–13: "If you then, though you are evil, know how to give good gifts to your children, how much more will your Father in heaven give the Holy Spirit to those who ask him!" Aware of the wretchedness of his life for the first time in years, panic stricken at the horrible sins he had committed, these words penetrated his heart with a piercing hope. With the lunge of a falling man desperate for any handhold, John grasped for some shred of faith big enough to float his sinking life. Were these words really true? Did God's forgiveness really encompass a murderous slave driver like him?

The sodden, battered cabin of the sinking ship became a place of conversion as real as that of St. Paul upon the Damascus Road. Paraphrased from his own writings his conclusion went like this, "The more I looked at what Jesus had done on the cross, the more He met my case exactly. I needed someone or something to stand between a righteous God and my sinful self ... and I found such a one in the New Testament." Once he understood, however dimly, God's great work was done. Newton renounced his past and embraced God's grace.

He wrote about it later in his diary,

Amazing grace, (how sweet the sound)
  That saved a wretch like me!
I once was lost, but now am found

Was blind, but now I see.
'Twas grace that taught my heart to fear,
    And grace my fears relieved.
How precious did that grace appear
    The hour I first believed.
Through many dangers, toils and snares,
    I have already come;
'Tis grace hath brought me safe thus far,
    And grace will lead me home.[34]

QUESTIONS FOR DISCUSSION

1. Why do you think the Bible is the Word of God? What does "Word of God" mean?

2. Several biblical stories are used in this chapter to show that "nothing is too hopeless for God." What other events in the Bible demonstrate this truth?

3. What do you think is God's purpose in the vision of Ezekiel 37:1–14? What present day applications can you find?

4. Jesus told the parable of the wise and foolish builders in Matthew 7:24–27. How is God's Word like a foundation?

5. The author says one of God's strategies for faith building is (a) God takes you to a valley, (b) God asks you a question, and (c) God asks you to apply his Word. What valley has helped you grow the most in your own walk with God?

NOTES

1. John 1:1
2. John 1:3–4
3. Hebrews 1:3

4. John 1:14
5. Hebrews 4:12–13
6. Genesis 1:2
7. Ezekiel 37
8. Acts 2
9. The following account, based on Ezekiel 1 and 37 is liberally laced with imagination. The words are different. We hope the truths of the story are the same.
10. Ezekiel 2:4
11. John 11:40
12. Isaiah 55:9
13. John 11:25
14. Luke 24:5–7
15. 2 Corinthians 4:8–9
16. Jeremiah 31:33
17. Genesis 12:2ff
18. John 3:17; italics added
19. Ezekiel 37:11–14, italics added
20. 1 John 1:1–2
21. Mark 4:39
22. John 11:43–44
23. Colossians 1:15–17
24. 1 Peter 1:25
25. Hebrews 4:12–13
26. Isaiah 55:10–11
27. John 5:6
28. Ephesians 1:17–20
29. Matthew 26:38
30. Romans 10:8–10
31. 1 Corinthians 15:9
32. The story of John Newton's life is taken from John Pollock's, *Amazing Grace* (San Francisco: Harper & Row Publishers, 1981).
33. Pollock, 12–13
34. Pollock, 1

3

God Is Speaking through Healing and Suffering

Hebrews 5:7–10; 13:6, 8

"Do you still have that room there at the Gospel Trumpet Company with the crutches and other displays of divine healing?" It was in January of 1994. The caller on the phone used the old name for Warner Press. He was an elder minister in the Church of God who perhaps had actually been in that room in which crutches and braces hung on the walls, the souvenirs of Church of God minister E. E. Byrum. Brother Byrum traveled widely across the nation preaching divine healing. The crutches and braces in his office were given him by those who had been healed.

"No," I answered my caller. I brought him up to date briefly on the many remodelings Warner Press has undergone. I thought, after he hung up, about other changes the Church of God has experienced. To my knowledge there are no such rooms any more. It is a graphic example of a gradual but notable doctrinal shift within the past generation: the rethinking of divine (miraculous) healing and suffering in the Christian life.

DO WE STILL BELIEVE AND TEACH
DIVINE HEALING?

Yes. Most Christians I know do still believe in divine healing. We acknowledge that all healing comes from God, therefore all healing is "divine." But we also believe that God still heals miraculously as the direct answer to faith-believing prayer, without the aid of any accompanying means.

Scriptural Support

We cannot explain how prayer for healing works, but we know it makes a difference. An editorial appeared in the Indianapolis Star on January 26, 1989, titled, "Power of Prayer." It commented on a report in the Journal of the American Medical Association stating that hospitalized patients who had other people praying for them experienced fewer medical complications.[1] Such reports only confirm the Scriptures from Genesis to Revelation, which abound with promises of God's healing intent. "I am the Lord who heals you,"[2] and "by his wounds we are healed,"[3] are two favorite examples. When Jesus walked into the synagogue in Nazareth, he read from the scroll of Isaiah the prophet, proclaiming his own mission and power to carry it out, "The Spirit of the Lord is on me, because he has anointed me to preach good news to the poor. He has sent me to proclaim freedom for the prisoners and recovery of sight for the blind, to release the oppressed, to proclaim the year of the Lord's favor."[4] The gospels overflow with eyewitness accounts of Christ's healing desire and power. Luke, himself a doctor, reports on the woman with the bleeding hemorrhage who touched the hem of Jesus' clothing and was miraculously restored.[5] Space does not permit a listing of all those healed of fevers, blindness, deafness, muteness, demons, leprosy, and epilepsy. They surely rejoiced with the psalmist, "Praise the Lord, O my soul, and forget not all his benefits. He forgives all my sins and heals all my diseases."[6]

48

Contemporary Evidence

Yes, we do believe miraculous healing still takes place today.

Hebrews 13:6, 8 declares,
Hence we say confidently,
"The Lord is my helper, I will not be afraid.
What can man do to me?
... [for] Jesus Christ is the same yesterday, today, and forever."

One of the most popular features in a recent *Vital Christianity* was a selection of testimonies by those who have received divine (miraculous) healing.

Joyce Calhoun wrote,

> From the time I began talking, no one could understand me. By the time I was six, my parents had become so accustomed to my method of communication that they were shocked when the school refused to enroll me; I would have to attend a special school where I might learn to speak understandably.
>
> My father and mother had recently been converted and were attending the revival at First Church of God in Elyria, Ohio, near where we lived. The speaker preached on divine healing that night, and my parents took me to the altar, where I was anointed with oil and prayed for.
>
> During the ride home one of my brothers exclaimed, "Listen, listen! Joyce is talking!" I was talking as plainly and clearly as anyone. I am still thanking God for my healing, for Christian parents, and for ministers who preach God's Word.[7]

Herman Richardson recalled,

> In the middle of the night I awoke with a severe pain in my left kidney. A stone was lodged in the tube leading to the kidney, and surgery was planned. Then I

began to hemorrhage. I was put into intensive care and my family was called.

My pastor, Vernon Roop and his wife, Mary, came to pray with me. Before prayer I asked that they not ask God to heal me but that God's will would be done. A wonderful calm and peace filled me. The Roops offered a short prayer.

Soon after they left, I felt something go over my whole body, and I knew God had healed me. The doctors confirmed that the bleeding had stopped and also that the stone was gone. Several years have passed now. Only God knows what happened to that stone.[8]

Nathan Smith, interviewed in the December 1993 *Vital Christianity*[9] was asked, "I know you have battled cancer [multiple myeloma, a rare bone cancer that is usually fatal within four years] for several years. Yet in spite of setbacks you still are able to continue life with a positive attitude. To what do you credit your victory over this illness, and how has it changed your life?

He answered, "I think my faith—and scripture.... My first prayer when I learned I had cancer was, 'God, may your name be glorified.' ...We decided to count our blessings from the very beginning. Looking at the blessings and trying to find joy in the midst of pain—I think those were important things."

His wife, Ann, commented, "We made two major decisions from the beginning. We said, 'We will begin our journey with cancer by counting our blessings.' The second decision we made was not to hide. We would be open and honest about both the good and the bad, the pain and the joy. After six and a half years with cancer, we believe those decisions had to come from the Lord."

Problems

Some people have difficulty in believing in miraculous healing. Why? Many factors contribute to this, such as the embarrassing excesses and sensationalism of television evangelists and the advancement and ready availability of modern medicine. We must also face the unpleasant fact that some of us, in teaching miraculous healing, have been dogmatic and hurtful toward those who are not healed. We make character judgments about either their faith or their Christian experience. Such behavior is not Christlike and has caused extraordinary emotional and spiritual damage to many wonderful Christians.

Why does this happen? In most churches that teach miraculous healing, there has been the tendency to create a formula by which such healing will come. Often James 5:13–15 is quoted, claiming especially, "the prayer offered in faith will make the sick person well; the Lord will raise him up." Many times Jesus said, in one form or another, "according to your faith will it be done to you." The formula then includes this: if you aren't healed, your faith is at fault.

Pastor Wayne Burch says, "I have yet to see a sure formula that will produce 'miracle' healing. We receive many blessings and privileges from God by simply living an obedient, disciplined life. We stray grossly from the faith, however, when we attempt to legislate those privileges into 'rights' and expect God to shower them upon us at the time of our choosing. God doesn't respond to such contrived manipulating tactics."[10] Thankfully, I personally have seen very little of this un-Christlike behavior.

Yet even when the unhealed person is surrounded by a congregation of loving, prayerful people, he or she often struggles with a feeling of spiritual failure (if I had more faith God would heal me), worthlessness (there must be something wrong with me or God would heal me), or cynicism (God is far away and doesn't care about me). What does the Bible teach about the significant numbers of deeply committed Christians who are not miraculously healed and obviously neither lack faith nor harbor unforgiven sin?

Foremost among those who have not escaped pain or death is Jesus Christ, "Who, being in very nature God, did not consider equality with God something to be grasped, but made himself nothing, taking the very nature of a servant, being made in human likeness. And being found in appearance as a man, he humbled himself and became obedient to death–even death on a cross! Therefore God exalted him to the highest place and gave him the name that is above every name."[11] A more thought-provoking passage in Hebrews 5:7–10 says that Jesus learned obedience from what he suffered; and in spite of his suffering, claims his prayers and petitions (with loud cries and tears) were heard because of his submission.[12]

THE NATURE OF CHRISTIANITY

Let us again examine the nature of our beliefs about Jesus Christ and the faith he teaches us. Is Christianity a religion of perfect health, unblighted happiness, and a high standard of living? This may be an attractive belief system, but biblical evidence fails to support this view. The more I study the life of Christ and the teachings of the scriptures, the more I am coming to believe that Christianity is a religion of suffering and survival, brokenness and healing, and finding peace through pain.

Does Christianity Really Teach that All Christians Will Be Healthy, Wealthy, and Wise?

The God-wants-you-to-be-wealthy cult desecrates Christianity and mocks the suffering of Jesus Christ. Here are at least three reasons:

1. This teaching separates the human race into groups: the "haves" from the "have-nots." It implies that those who receive material blessings must be God's favored, and that those who don't must be sinful. Taken to its inevitable conclusion, such teaching supports obviously selfish and provincial views: that God loves North America more than the rest of the world, for example. Why? Because we have better health care and a higher standard of living than most of the rest of the world.

In the realm of physical healing, the God-wants-you-to-be-wealthy teaching screeches to the same awful conclusions. If one holds to the belief that those with enough faith will always be physically healed, then those who are healed are rewarded as being "faithful." Those who are not healed are defamed and criticized as being sinful, faithless, or somehow unworthy of God's favor.

2. This teaching misses the point of the Gospel altogether, which is, "A man's life does not consist in the abundance of his possessions."[13] We are constantly tempted to judge the success of our walk with God by the number of our prayers visibly answered and the material blessings received. Worse, we judge each other by the same criteria, when no one can possibly know another's heart.

I remember sitting under the teaching of Dr. Boyce Blackwelder, eminent New Testament scholar in the Anderson University School of Theology, when we discussed this very subject. I will not forget his impassioned statement: "There's something greater than divine healing: submission to the will of God." To demand that God heal every illness for ourselves and those we know impoverishes the deep truths of God who has allowed suffering and even martyrdom. "Going a little farther, [Jesus] fell with his face to the ground and prayed, 'My Father, if it is possible, may this cup be taken from me. Yet not as I will, but as you will.' "[14]

Hebrews 11:36ff eloquently pleads for the unnamed faithful who "faced jeers and flogging, while still others were chained and put in prison. They were stoned; they were sawed in two; they were put to death by the sword. They went about in sheepskins and goatskins, destitute, persecuted and mistreated–the world was not worthy of them." By the time John's Revelation was written, the Christian church had been ushered into the fiery persecution at the hand of Rome. Thousands, perhaps hundreds of thousands, perished while grasping an unshakable faith in Christ.

The twentieth century has not proved to be kinder or gentler. Christians around the world recount experiences of imprisonment, torture, and unspeakable atrocities. As they share their experiences of suffering the same truth always comes to light: Christianity works in the deepest hell. The stories rarely relate that God whisks the believer away from the pain. What we learn is that there is a deeper message.

Among the many Christians who endured the ghastly torment of Hitler's concentration camps because they had assisted Jews to escape the Nazi juggernaut were two Dutch sisters, Corrie and Betsie ten Boom. Their story is told in The Hiding Place, first a book and then a major motion picture. In this gripping tale, Corrie recalls her family's decimation and the brutalizing experiences she and Betsie endured as they were shuffled from one death camp to another. In those horrifying places, which Betsie did not survive, Corrie discovers the real truth of the cross: that in the midst of pain the truth of Christianity's love and grace finally stand out in clear relief. She observes,

> But as the rest of the world grew stranger, one thing became increasingly clear. And that was the reason the two of us were here. Why others should suffer we were not shown. As for us, from morning until lights-out, whenever we were not in ranks for roll call, our Bible was the center of an ever-widening circle of help and hope. Like waifs clustered around a blazing fire, we gathered about it, holding out our hearts to its warmth and light. The blacker the night around us grew, the brighter and truer and more beautiful burned the world of God. "Who shall separate us from the love of Christ? Shall tribulation, or distress, or persecution, or famine, or nakedness, or peril, or sword?... Nay, in all these things we are more than conquerors through him that loved us."
>
> I would look about us as Betsie read, watching the light leap from face to face. More than conquerors.... It was not a wish. It was a fact. We knew it, we experienced it minute by minute—poor, hated, hungry. We are more than conquerors. Not "we shall be." We are! Life in Ravensbruck took place on two separate levels, mutually impossible. One, the observable, external life, grew every day more horrible. The other, the life we lived with God, grew daily better, truth upon truth, glory upon glory.[15]

3. The God-wants-you-to-be-wealthy cult insults and belittles the human spirit, created in God's image. How could a person's soul be satisfied with material possessions and good health? They are impermanent holdings rooted only in mortality and not in grace. Christ died to save us from the material world and its insistent claims upon our souls. His gifts, in fact, transcend the physical. To rely on the physical contradicts the Master's values.

Paul writes about his experience with praying for divine healing in 2 Corinthians 12:7–10, "To keep me from becoming conceited because of these surpassingly great revelations, there was given me a thorn in my flesh, a messenger of Satan, to torment me. Three times I pleaded with the Lord to take it away from me. But he said to me, 'My grace is sufficient for you, for my power is made perfect in weakness.' Therefore I will boast all the more gladly about my weaknesses, so that Christ's power may rest on me. That is why, for Christ's sake, I delight in weaknesses, in insults, in hardships, in persecutions, in difficulties. For when I am weak, then I am strong."

Andrew Wyerman recalls, "I remember the witness of Bishop Lajos Ordass of the Lutheran Church in Hungary to a small group gathered at the Lutheran World Federation Assembly in Minneapolis in 1957. As bishop he protested the communist regime's confiscation of church schools and was imprisoned for twenty months. Later, he was under arrest for six years. He was a tall stately man, and I can still see his ashen face as he quietly told his story. 'They placed me in solitary confinement. It was a tiny cell perhaps six feet by eight feet with no windows and sound-proofed. They hoped to break down my resistance by isolating me from all sensory perceptions. They thought I was alone. They were wrong. The Risen Christ was present in that room, and in communion with him I was able to prevail.' "[16]

Christianity is a Religion of Identification, Not Separation

Christ unites across gender, race, and class. False religion separates people into a hierarchy of groups. Christianity is a religion of identification with others, not separation from them. While other religions teach separation from the world and its pain, God in Christ so identified with our world that he became one of us.[17] This "great reduction," in the phrase of Calvin Miller, not only somehow satisfies the requirements of justice on the part of God, but uniquely qualifies God in our eyes to understand our situation. "We see Jesus, who was made a little lower than the angels ... so that by the grace of God he might taste death for everyone."[18]

From our limited viewpoint, we can explain only partially why Christ came to earth: because he loves us, to become the substitute sacrifice for us and bear on our behalf the weight and retribution for our sins, and because it was God's will. Ultimately our explanations patter against the greatness of God like pebbles against Mount Everest. There is no suitable explanation within the limits of human logic for the transcendent Almighty God to stoop to such degradation and humiliation.

As we probe the wonderful depths of these truths, let us not miss the fact that suffering was an apparently indispensable ingredient, both wonderful and horrible. "In bringing many sons to glory, it was fitting that God, for whom and through whom everything exists, should make the author of their salvation perfect through suffering…. Since the children have flesh and blood, *he too shared in their humanity* so that by his death he might destroy him who holds the power of death—that is, the devil—and free those who all their lives were held in slavery by their fear of death…. Because he himself suffered when he was tempted, he is able to help those who are being tempted."[19]

We are instructed to follow this divine pattern. "This is how we know what love is: Christ laid down his life for us. And we ought to lay down our lives for our brothers."[20] In other words, because Christ identified with us, we are to identify with others. Of course, our identification with others cannot in any way provide salvation, except insofar as our compassionate caring will attract them to the one who calls us his friends.

Christianity Unites Because God Identifies with All People

God's total identification with humankind is flabbergasting. God becomes a man and dies for everyone so some will be saved. "For God so loved the world that he gave his one and only Son, that *whoever* believes in him shall not perish but have eternal life."[21] Many individuals or groups throughout human history have tried to create a "chosen people." None but Christ has made the entry point "whoever."

Hitler had a dream to unite the world by creating a super race, people just like him who believed what he believed. Through their alleged genetic superiority they would multiply until only their race was left. His plan was to weed out the undesirables, to divide the acceptable from the unacceptable. He followed his vision with chilling efficiency. This hellish program led to the barbarous slaughter of more than six million Jews during World War II.

Even religious organizations with the best of intentions have divided people into groups. Look at the Pharisees and other Jewish leaders of Jesus' day. Since they were physical descendants of Abraham, to whom God gave the covenant in which he pledged himself to his people, we can understand their persective.

But by the time Jesus arrived they had painstakingly developed an elaborate system of rules and rituals that in fact separated them from the "unrighteous" masses. They observed a strict caste system that kept them from even traveling through neighboring countries like Samaria, whose people they taught were inferior half-breeds. They looked down upon "ordinary" people, a fact Jesus used liberally and pointedly to illustrate his teaching.

Sadly, the Pharisees' efforts to create a "chosen people" were miles off base and made God altogether inaccessible to ordinary folks. Their strategy was to divide and separate. Jesus' strategy was to identify with and encourage. What is our strategy?

In many of our congregations we have separated the "healed" and the "unhealed." Those who pray for healing but are not healed carry the burden of thoughtless comments for years. Within my own family there are members who were told in so many words that "God hasn't healed you because you don't have enough faith," and "Because you have not been healed there must be unforgiven sin in your life. Repent."

"Doesn't God separate people into groups?" we ask. Yes. Jesus himself recounted the judgment day scenario from Matthew 25:31–46 in which all the nations of the world will be divided into righteous and unrighteous. The writer of 1 John 2 pulls no punches when he says Christians must not become entangled with or enamored by the world. The key difference in God's method of choosing and human attempts to do so lies at the point of entry. God makes membership in the family of God available to everyone.[22] Many of us don't.

Christianity Unites Us by Embracing Reality

We are forever endeared to Jesus Christ for walking the road of suffering and death ahead of us. Jesus' steady persistence in facing the worst that life has to offer ennobles our daily lives. The fact that Jesus lived as a human being elevates human existence. That he went to weddings hallows marriage. His sadness at the death of Lazarus lifts human grief, and his tears sanctify sorrow. Look again at his strategy: he constantly went to the down and out, the disenfranchised, the outcasts. He gave his best sermons to women of ill repute. He lavished attention on fishermen. He welcomed children. He purposely visited neighborhoods snubbed by the yuppies of his day.

And just why do you think he did these things? To identify with common, ordinary people who hadn't the least hope of being chosen most likely to succeed. He was saying, "It's okay to be human. It's all right to be sick. Even if your family is an embarrassment, you won't be an embarrassment to God. Crippled? It's what's in your heart that counts. Unattractive? See the advice for cripples. Anyone can provide an acceptable home for the Son of God since God lives in the human heart.

Dumping the Stigmas

Remember the man blind from birth?[23] Social convention of the day assumed the blindness was caused by sin, either that of the man himself or of his parents. Jesus cleared it up when he said, "Neither this man nor his parents sinned, *but this happened so that the work of God might be displayed in his life.*" Think of that! Jesus was planning to use a "second rate" citizen to demonstrate the power and glory of God. When you have God, you have everything. The gift of sight this man received was secondary to meeting Christ.

The human spirit can be victorious and whole even when jailed inside a paraplegic body. We do not deny pain. We learn to use it.

If we insist on praying that every difficulty and illness be removed from our lives, we will lose one of life's most profound lessons.

Frederick Buechner, in his book, *Now and Then*, has a section on his comparison of the teachings of Buddha and Jesus Christ, a topic he wrestled with when he was teaching at Phillips-Exeter Academy.

> Finally, lest students of comparative religions be tempted to believe that to compare them is to discover that at their hearts all religions are finally one and that it thus makes little difference which one you choose; you have only to place side by side Buddha and Christ themselves.
>
> Buddha sits enthroned beneath the Bo tree in the lotus position. His lips are faintly parted in the smile of one who has passed beyond every power in earth or heaven to touch him. "He who loves fifty has fifty woes, he who loves ten has ten woes, he who loves none has no woes," he has said. His eyes are closed.
>
> Christ on the other hand stands in the Garden of Gethsemane, angular, beleaguered. His face is lost in shadows so that you can't even see his lips, and before all the powers in earth or heaven he is powerless. "This is my commandment, that you love one another as I have loved you," he has said. His eyes are also closed. The difference seems to me this. The suffering that Buddha's eyes close out is the suffering of the world that Christ's eyes close in and hallow. It is an extraordinary difference.[24]

THREE HELPFUL PRINCIPLES

As one contemplates the place of suffering and healing in the Christian life, I find it helpful to consider the following principles:

On the Way to Life There Is Death

"Unless a kernel of wheat falls to the gound and dies, it remains only a single seed. But if it dies, it produces many seeds."[25]

The diminutive nun whose likeness the world instantly recognizes as Mother Teresa has become an amazing symbol of hope. Practically single-handedly, it seems, she established an outpost of compassion in one of the bleakest and most terrifying cities in the world: Calcutta, the "black hole." Her order, the Missionaries of Charity, have now established ministries around the globe, in many of the world's largest cities.[26] They are invariably planted smack dab in the middle of the most crime-infested, miserable ghettos of humanity.

As a Yugoslavian schoolgirl, Mother Teresa gave herself to Christ and served as a nun for some twenty years. It was while she was teaching at the Loreto Convent School in Calcutta that the second great break in Mother Teresa's life took place; the call within a call, as she puts it. She had occasion to go into some of the very poorest streets of Calcutta … and suddenly realized that she belonged there, not in her Loreto Convent with its pleasant garden, eager schoolgirls, congenial colleagues, and rewarding work. She had to wait for some two years to be released from the vows she had already taken in order to be able to go back into the world, there to take even stricter vows of her own devising…. When at last her release came, she stepped out with a few rupees in her pocket, made her way to the poorest, most wretched quarter of the city, found lodging there, gathered together a few abandoned children, and began her ministry of love.[27]

Those who spend time with Mother Teresa immediately notice her reverence for human life. Observing one helper gingerly and at arm's length cleaning a wounded man, the stench of whose rotting flesh filled the room, she gently inserted herself, embraced the man closely, and spoke to him gently while cleaning his sores. Every person is God in disguise, she admonished, and worthy of reverent care.

> Make us worthy, Lord, to serve our sisters and broth-
> ers throughout the world who live and die in poverty
> and hunger.
>
> Give them through our hands this day their daily
> bread, and by our understanding love, give peace and
> joy.[28]

Her aim was to alleviate suffering of a few people by doing what
one or two people could do, bring them in off the street to die with
dignity. She is fond of saying that what the poor need, even more
than food and clothing and shelter, is to be wanted. Welfare serves
a purpose. Christians serve a person. The great personalities of our
time—not celebrities from Tinsel Town, but truly great people—
have rarely dreamed of starting a movement to change the world.
They have begun ministering where they are with what they had.

Malcolm Muggeridge writes of her with awe following a personal interview,

> She, a nun, rather slightly built, with a few rupees in
> her pocket; not particularly clever, or particularly gifted
> in the arts of persuasion. Just with this Christian love
> shining about her; in her heart and on her lips. Just pre-
> pared to follow her Lord, and … regard every derelict
> left to die in the streets as him; to hear in the cry of
> every abandoned child, even in the tiny squeak of the
> discarded fetus, the cry of the Bethlehem child; to rec-
> ognize in every leper's stumps the hands which once
> touched sightless eyes and made them see.[29]

Experience Matters

"Because he himself suffered when he was tempted, he is able to
help those who are being tempted."[30]

When it comes to surgery, everyone wants a surgeon who is
experienced. We may laugh at cartoons in which the dim-witted
doctors lift up organs they have removed from patients and ask,
"Does anybody know what this is?" Of course, in real life, it's not
funny.

Too often in the church we have been eager to counsel those whose problems we have never experienced. At times we who "preach the truth" have been almost crass in our determination to get a point across. Those who have actually experienced the loss or the cancer or the abuse—they cannot only offer sympathy but empathy. Experience gives one the right to offer advice.

A Personal Experience with Depression

Years ago I preached a series of messages about "Killer Atttitudes." I dealt with problems such as anger and self-pity. One of these messages addressed depression. It seemed simple at the time: defeat depression by disciplining yourself, staying close to God, and being positive. It was not bad advice. But I had no idea what I was talking about. I knew nothing of the insidious, often invisible beginnings of depression, much less the incapacitating years during which one's faith erodes and hope flickers, then dies.

Then, even though I had every reason to be victorious, it happened to me. I was the pastor of a large and "successful" congregation. I had a wonderful family and a gifted, warm, and supportive wife. The first signs of depression were barely visible, in retropsect, in 1987. I stopped laughing. I began to respond to small events as though they were catastrophes. My ability to "go with the flow" thinned to a trickle. The harder I prayed the more distant God seemed to be. All I wanted to do was leave. The thought of never preaching again filled me with delight. I fantasized about spending the rest of my life on some forgotten stretch of beach on a desert island, where no phones rang and no committees met. In May, 1990, I couldn't continue. I asked the Church Council for a three-month leave, and it was graciously granted. They wisely stipulated that during that time I receive professional counsel. I said goodbye to Karon and my family and drove south for a month alone.

Daily I paced the Gulf Coast beaches of Mississippi. I was in crisis. I had told a friend in Alabama a week earlier that everything I believed was up for grabs. I wasn't a college kid now, but a middle-aged pastor. Questions that my mind told me should have been answered years before now hammered at my heart. Long-repressed anger surged into the light. Burnout, midlife crisis, depression—

these clinical sounding terms cannot describe the stark hopelessness of the dark night of the soul that suffocated me. Whenever I thought about the church I was gripped by feelings of anger and rage. How could I possibly consider continuing in ministry? I would ruin the church.

One morning the long-silent heavens cracked open. I recognized the Voice that spoke my name and directed me to a verse in Mark: "You are my son, whom I love; with you I am well pleased."[31] A shaft of light pierced my darkness. Could it be that God actually was still planning to use me? Was I still usable? Hadn't I disqualified myself with imperfection and doubt? Again the Voice spoke, and again from scripture: "Satan has asked to sift you as wheat. But I have prayed for you, that your faith may not fail. And when you have turned back, strengthen your brothers."[32]

I returned to North Anderson Church of God that September. Although my healing was only beginning, I spent the first five Sundays sharing what I had already learned. My messages obviously hit some nerves. While our regular tape sales of Sunday services were modestly brisk, now people were buying them by the tens and twenties and sending them all over the country! Later, when we moved to California and I began my work as state coordinator, I found myself unusually qualified to counsel pastors and congregations who themselves were going through difficulties.

I won't use that message again, the one which flippantly suggested three quick steps to beat depression. (Life is rarely helped with three, five, or even ten quick steps.) What I can and do share is the depth of God's love for me—and for you. My flaws and failures have not kept God at arm's length, nor will your problems or illness keep him from you.

Because of my pain, I am useful to God in new ways! What a marvelous serendipity! Formerly judged by many pastors to be unapproachable, my problems broke down the barriers between us. I found in my own heart a new appreciation for every person who serves God faithfully. I hope I have become a more supportive Christian, encouraging, counseling pastors who are too busy, urging churches and boards to protect their leaders. In short, experience has made the difference. I would never hope for anyone to undergo such a wrenching experience. I wouldn't want to go through it again! But I am richer for it.

Suffering Prepares Us for Ministry

"For this reason he had to be made like his brothers in every way, in order that he might become a merciful and faithful high priest."[33]

The experiences God providentially allows in our lives can springboard us to places we could never have served before. Just as my own bout with depression and burnout has enabled me to minister to others in the same boat, those who survive illnesses, crises, and abuse become much more useful than before in helping others.

Most of us know about support groups that operate by this premise. Alcoholics Anonymous, perhaps the first such group, has helped millions of people. The proliferation of such groups is stupefying. At times it seems every problem anybody ever had now has a support group meeting with "anonymous" after it (*Overeaters' Anonymous* and *Co-Dependents Anonymous*, for example).

Why are they so popular? They are meeting a need of the heart no theology can meet. When you're in the waiting room while your spouse is undergoing cancer surgery, there's something wonderfully comforting about having someone strike up a conversation and say, "Your husband has cancer and my husband has cancer, but God still loves us and we can get through this." When you're recovering from the death of a family member, there is terrific affinity for someone who can lovingly offer these words, "Your daughter may have died, and my son committed suicide, but life can still be worth living because God still is in charge."

Do you think that at times the unchurched stay away from our congregations because they never hear, "You are a sinner and I am a sinner but God forgives all sinners who ask him to." What do they hear? Can they identify with us? Are we too perfect? Or do we pretend that we're perfect because that's what we've been taught we must do?

Father Damien DeVeuster

It seems ironic that heavenly Molokai, one of the seven idyllic islands of the Hawaiian group, should have become a leper colony in the 1800s. Partly as a carryover from the ideas of those who lived in biblical times, a leper was considered unclean, a person unfit for "clean" society. For many years these unfortunate people were dispatched to Molokai where they were left to die in the most horrible conditions.

Women and children as well as men were forced to jump from the boats and swim ashore. Waiting for them on the beaches were scores of lepers who would beat them and steal whatever clothing they had brought. Women were often raped repeatedly in broad daylight. There was no order. There were no doctors. There were no clinics. There was nothing at all except anarchy and horror.

Damien, as a young priest, felt that when Jesus said we shall be witnesses in Judea and Samaria to the ends of the earth, it included Molokai. Nobody else, it seems, had figured that out yet. But Damien had. He went to his bishop and asked permission to move to the island and be with the people and do what he could. The bishop loved this young priest, a man of great promise, and he tried to argue him out of it. It didn't seem fitting that this young man with so much potential should throw himself away in that forsaken place.

But Damien persuaded the bishop and soon thereafter boarded that horrible ship of death to Molokai. In the early weeks there he was often dreadfully sick at his stomach as he moved among the people and saw the abominable conditions under which they were living. It was all he could do to force himself to stay in spite of his strong intention. But he went to work. First of all, he found a source of fresh water up in the mountain. He was able to build a little system to bring the fresh water down to the village, in time becoming the colony's first sanitation system. He showed the lepers how to build little houses to replace the flimsy shacks and hovels in which they were living. He built a clinic. Although he had little medical knowledge, nevertheless he could at least dress their sores and give them comfort.

Damien helped them build a small chapel where he preached

each Sunday. Over the years they became accustomed to seeing him enter the pulpit, cross himself, and begin the sermon with these same words: "You lepers know that God the Father loves you." He then would preach a message full of hope, joy, and life.

Several years went by in this way, until one Sunday morning he went into the pulpit, crossed himself, and said, "We lepers know that God the Father loves us." It was everyone's first indication that Damien had contracted leprosy himself. He continued to pour himself out in his ministry of love until he died, a leper among the lepers whom he loved and who loved him. Father Damien died in 1889 at the age of forty-nine.[34]

"For this reason [Jesus] had to be made like his brothers in every way, in order that he might become a merciful and faithful high priest."[35] Surely we cannot save anyone. In what ways, however, can we identify with them? It's a thought-provoking question.

QUESTIONS FOR DISCUSSION

1. Define "divine" healing according to your understanding of scripture.

2. How do you reconcile what the church has taught you about divine (miracle) healing and the Christian who has been anointed for healing but is not healed?

3. How do you react to the statement: "Christianity is a religion of suffering and survival, brokenness and healing, and finding peace through pain." Is this biblical? Why or why not?

4. How does the church divide people into groups? Do you perceive this as good or bad?

5. What can one learn through suffering that cannot be learned any other way?

NOTES

1. Reported by Wayne Burch in "God Does the Healing," *Vital Christianity* 111 (November 1991), 22.

2. Exodus 15:26

3. Isaiah 53:5

4. Luke 4:18

5. Luke 13:11

6. Psalm 103:2–3

7. "Testimonies of Healing," *Vital Christianity* 111 (November 1991): 26.

8. *Vital Christianity* 111 (November 1991): 26.

9. *113* December 1993: 22–23.

10. 22.

11. Philippians 2:5–9

12. "During the days of Jesus' life on earth, he offered up prayers and petitions with loud cries and tears to the one who could save him from death, and he was heard because of his reverent submission. Although he was a son, he learned obedience from what he suffered and, once made perfect, he became the source of eternal salvation for all who obey him and was designated by God to be high priest in the order of Melchizedek" (Hebrews 5:7–10).

13. Luke 12:15

14. Matthew 26:39

15. Corrie ten Boom, *The Hiding Place* (Washington Depot, Conn: Chosen Books, 1971), 177–78.

16. "He Lives Today," *The Pastor's Story File* (April 1987) 5.

17. Romans 8:3

18. Hebrews 2:9

19. Hebrews 2:10–18, italics added

20. 1 John 3:16

21. John 3:16, italics added

22. John 3:16

23. John 9

24. Frederick Buechner, *Now and Then* (San Francisco: Harper & Row: 1983), 53–54.

25. John 12:24

26. By 1990 there were more than seventy centers around the world, including one for adult AIDS victims in New York City. Forty years after launching her work, Missionaries of Charity now incorporates some 3,000 sisters and 500 brothers. More than three million people from seventy countries pray for and help provide resources. See Linda Carlson Johnson, *Mother Teresa: Protector of the Sick*, (New York: Blackbirch Press, 1991), 42, 56–58.

27. Malcolm Muggeridge, *Something Beautiful for God* (San Francisco: Harper & Row, 1971), 19.

28. Taken from a manual of devotion used by the *Missionaries of Charity*, Muggeridge, 39.

29. Muggeridge 22.

30. Hebrews 2:18

31. Mark 1:11

32. Luke 22:31–32

33. Hebrews 2:17

34. James F. Colainanni, editor, *Sunday Sermons Treasury of Illustrations* (Pleasantville, NJ: Voicings Publication: Pleasantville, 1982), 63–64.

35. Hebrews 2:17

4

God Is Speaking: Encourage One Another

Hebrews 10:24–25

It's amazing but true. Computers link us up to libraries across the country and around the world. Satellites beam us news as it happens from the most remote outposts of the globe. Surgeons perform micro surgery within the brain that was impossible a few years ago. Automobiles actually speak to us, telling us the fuel is low or the door is ajar. Technologies are catapulting us into a world described only in science fiction novels a few years ago.

But no matter how sophisticated our machines become, no matter how quickly we can access state of the art information, the emotional needs of people do not change from one generation to the next. These heart needs can never be satisfied with knowledge, science, or technology. In the 1980s President George Bush urged citizens of the United States to make ours a "kinder, gentler nation." We long for this to happen, especially as crime escalates. We cannot imagine another time in history as bad as ours. But people in other times have made the same plea.

"These are troubled times." wrote a businessman in the 1940s. "The world is full of strife and heartache. Men and women everywhere seek peace of mind and heart, and wish desperately that they as individuals could do something toward lifting the heavy blanket of gloom and fear that oppresses mankind.... More than anything else, the world needs the healing influence of a great surge of simple kindheartedness."[1]

This author offers a thousand suggestions about ways to encourage people. He is not a Christian and is long-since dead, yet his words strike a nerve today in the 1990s, decades later.

A Tragic Event Sparks Love

A third man writes of a tragic incident that helped propel him into a career that has made his name a household word in the United States today.

> On my first day as an assistant professor of education at the University of Southern California, I entered the classroom with a great deal of anxiety. My large class responded to my awkward smile and brief greetings with silence. For a few moments I fussed with my notes. Then I started my lecture, stammering: no one seemed to be listening.
>
> At that moment of panic I noticed in the fifth row a poised, attentive young woman in a summer dress. Her skin was tanned, her brown eyes were clear and alert, her hair was golden. Her animated expression and warm smile were an invitation for me to go on. When I'd say something, she would nod, or say, "O yes!" and write it down. She emanated the comforting feeling that she cared about what I was trying so haltingly to do.
>
> I began to speak directly to her, and my confidence and enthusiasm returned. After a while I risked looking about. The other students had begun listening and taking notes. This stunning young woman had pulled me through.
>
> After class, I scanned the roll to find her name: Liani. Her papers, which I read over the subsequent weeks, were written with creativity, sensitivity, and a delicate sense of humor.

I had asked all my students to visit my office during the semester, and I awaited Liani's visit with special interest. I wanted to tell her how she had saved my first day, and encourage her to develop her qualities of caring and awareness.

Liani never came. About five weeks into the semester, she missed two weeks of classes. I asked the students seated around her if they knew why. I was shocked to learn that they did not even know her name. I thought of Schweitzer's poignant statement: "We are all so much together and yet we are all dying of loneliness."

I went to our dean of women. The moment I mentioned Liani's name, she winced, "Oh, I'm sorry, Leo," she said. "I thought you'd been told."

Liani had driven to Pacific Palisades, a lovely community near downtown Los Angeles where cliffs fall abruptly into the sea. There, shocked picnickers later reported, she jumped to her death.

Liani was 22 years old! And her God-given uniqueness was gone forever.

I called Liani's parents. From the tenderness with which Liani's mother spoke of her, I knew that she had been loved. But it was obvious to me that Liani had not felt loved.

"What are we doing?" I asked a colleague. "We're so busy teaching things. What's the value of teaching Liani to read, write, do arithmetic, if we taught her nothing of what she truly needed to know: how to live in joy, how to have a sense of personal worth and dignity?"

I decided to do something to help others who needed to feel loved. I would teach a course on love.[2]

And that's how Leo Buscaglia began his amazing career of teaching people how to love one another. He is known to millions today through his TV appearances, lectures, and such best-selling books as *Love*; *Living, Loving & Learning*; and *The Fall of Freddie the Leaf*.

The Acid Test

A fourth man, Jesus Christ, said it most eloquently, "Greater love has no one than this, that one lay down his life for his friends."[3] Jesus then carefully lived out this instruction, giving to us on the cross the ultimate encouragement that each of us is cherished by God. His years among us were brief but unforgettable. His words shoot like flaming arrows to set our hearts ablaze with this timeless truth: people are God's treasures. Not churches. Not institutions. Not doctrine. In Matthew 25 he teaches about the Judgment Day. From his own lips comes his description of the ultimate test by which God divides the chosen from the damned: how we have treated people.

> Then the King will say to those at his right hand, "Come, O blessed of my Father, inherit the kingdom prepared for you from the foundation of the world; for I was hungry and you gave me food, I was thirsty and you gave me drink, I was a stranger and you welcomed me, I was naked and you clothed me, I was sick and you visited me, I was in prison and you came to me." Then the righteous will answer him, "Lord, when did we see thee hungry and feed thee, or thirsty and give thee drink? And when did we see thee a stranger and welcome thee, or naked and clothe thee? And when did we see thee sick or in prison and visit thee?" And the King will answer them, "Truly, I say to you, as you did it to one of the least of these my brethren, you did it to me."[4]

No one has ever lived out the admonition better than Christ himself.

To live with the purpose of encouraging others is one of the hardest lessons for us to learn. We are so very self-centered, so selfish.

Even in the church?

Yes. Sometimes especially in the church.

Hidden Love Is a Tragedy

People do not benefit from unexpressed love. If love is not shown us, we are like empty automobiles with full gas cans beside us, unable to run. If love is not shown us, we are like starving men and women locked in a closet in the same room where a banquet table is loaded with delicious food we cannot eat. Mr. Buscaglia noted, when interviewing Liani's parents, that they in fact loved her. But she did not believe that she was loved. In Jesus' terms from Matthew 25, Liani was hungry but her parents somehow didn't feed her.

You Made Me What I Am

Bob Benson uses marriage as an analogy to explain our dependence on others in order to become all that we have the potential to become.

> During the first years of our marriage we were struggling through graduate school and pastoring tiny churches. We had two young sons and Peg was working part of the time. It was easy to get into some rather lively discussions about life in general and ours in particular. Sometimes she spoke so loudly that I even had to raise my voice to be heard.
>
> Sometimes I had to remind her of some of her faults and failures. This, of course, was always done in order to help. She always ended such family dialogue with the phrase, "You made me what I am!" The truth is that, at any point in marriage, you are in some way responsible for what the other partner is becoming. I think husbands and wives have a perfect right to say, "You are making me what I am."[5]

I find this concept both wonderful and shocking. It's wonderful because in my own marriage and family we have shared love and support, and we are growing into people who know how to give and receive love.

It is shocking because there are hundreds–maybe thousands–of people whom my life has touched but to whom I have shown no love. Hasn't my coldness, my insensitivity, my apathy helped make them what they are? It is possible that some people in my world about whom I complain the loudest and longest are the way they are partly because I "made them that way." Doesn't it follow that some people in our own congregations are the way they are because we have spent all of our lives complaining about them instead of encouraging them to be something different?

Jesus and his relationships offer a positive example. Take Peter, for instance. He was a diamond in the rough, and Jesus must have had pretty good vision to see any diamond at all. Peter was clumsy at relationships and had the uncanny knack of always saying the wrong thing. He promised more than he could possibly deliver and Jesus knew it. Yet during those three years of friendship and teaching, something about Jesus was rubbing off on Peter. Or, to be more accurate, we could say something about Jesus was rubbing off Peter's rough places. Jesus invested himself in this man. He "encouraged" him by believing in him again and again, even when Peter swore he'd never heard of him. After the resurrection and the birth of the church on the Day of Pentecost, a new Peter appeared. He was a diamond whose fire helped birth the church across the Mediterranean world. Jesus made him what he was.

GOD DOES NOT HIDE HIS LOVE

Here is a sweeping statement. See if you agree with it: most people's problems stem from this: they don't understand how much God loves them. Escalating crime and violence originate in the hearts of those who feel cheated by life. Wars drag on as nations and their leaders fight to gain power or prestige. Physical and sexual abuse proliferate among those who are themselves abused, hated, and mistreated.

If our violent citizens could only see that their deepest needs can be met through forgiveness; if our world's leaders could only grasp that the power and prestige they seek is available freely from Christ; if the abusers among us could only find in their mirrors a person worth loving; how peace would then grow in our world!

Why don't people understand how much God loves them? Has God hidden his love? No. Just the opposite, in fact. God himself has relentlessly pursued us from creation 'til now, revealing himself in countless ways.

GOD SHOWS US HIS LOVE

God places us in a fabulous world that appeals to all of our senses. Our eyes feast on the deep blue sky of a summer day. Great, fleecy clouds drift lazily by. The shade of the maples dances back and forth across the green lawn. Bright pink, white, and scarlet flowers blaze along the pathways. Butterflies pirouette like prima ballerinas, their wings a riot of color. Our mouths rejoice in the succulence of fresh peaches and strawberries in the spring. Our noses celebrate with the incomparable smell of bread baking in the oven. Our ears open to us the soaring symphonies of music, the melodies of Gershwin, Rachmaninoff, and Beethoven; to the piercing sweetness of a robin's spring song, or the haunting loneliness of a harmonica played by a campfire. Our bodies, chilled to the bone on a cold winter night, luxuriate in the steaming therapy of a hot bath.

God delights by filling our days with surprises. As someone observed, "Who else could make a brown cow that eats green grass give white milk and yellow butter?" A scientist observed that according to laws of aerodynamics, the bumblebee has insufficient wingspread to fly. But bumblebees, unaware of this shortcoming, just go ahead and fly anyway.

In Everyone God Sees Something Lovable

God's revelation is far richer than just the mortal world, fantastic as it is. From the beginning of recorded history (*i.e.*, the Bible), God's habit is to strike up relationships with whomever happens to be listening. He sees something of value in everyone: Adam and his regret for a barely remembered Eden. Samson's muscle-bound arrogance and deadly weakness. Noah waiting with tears in his eyes for the dove to return. David's exuberant dance of crazy joy around the Ark of the Covenant.[6]

Pastor Steve Birch explores this amazing inclination of God.

> Many years ago my Grandmother Birch died and left a few articles behind. There were very few things that she left because she knew mainly poverty here on earth. Her 'treasures' were in heaven. The Birch clan is a large family and all of the children wanted something that belonged to Grandma Birch. After each child chose an item, the rest of the junk (we did not realize everything was antiques) was sold at auction.
> My father bought an old spindle bed that had been in the family for well over one hundred years. He paid five dollars for it and I thought he was cheated. The bed was a horrible looking thing with white and green paint. My father paid an old man in our church to refinish the bed. He removed six or seven layers of paint and varnished the bed for twenty dollars. The bed is now one of the few pieces of furniture we own that is worth anything.... I am glad my father saw beyond the green and white paint to the beauty just below.[7]

The amazing thing about God is that God sees below the surface to recapture the real value in a life. Leslie Weatherhead states, "It is not so true to say that He loves the unlovable as to say that in every one He sees something lovable."

GOD TELLS US HE LOVES US

In communicating his love to us, God seemingly follows the advice of the southern preacher, who said, "Tell 'em that you're gonna tell 'em. Then tell 'em what it is you want to tell 'em. Then tell 'em what you've just told 'em!" God repeatedly proclaims, whispers, shouts, and bellows his love throughout the scriptures.

A Sample of Scriptural Encouragement

Deuteronomy 7:8 announces, "But it was because the Lord loved you and kept the oath he swore to your forefathers that he brought you out with a mighty hand and redeemed you from the land of slavery."

Isaiah 41:8–10:
"But you, O Israel, my servant,
Jacob, whom I have chosen,
　　you descendants of Abraham my friend,
　　I took you from the ends of the earth,
　　from its farthest corners I called you.
　I said, 'You are my servant';
I have chosen you and have not rejected you.
　So do not fear, for I am with you;
　　do not be dismayed,
　　for I am your God.' "

And again in Isaiah 49:14–16:
But Zion said, "The LORD has forsaken me,
　　the LORD has forgotten me."
"Can a mother forget the baby at her breast
　　and have no compassion on the child she has borne?
Though she may forget,
　I will not forget you!
See, I have engraved you on the palms of my hands;
　　your walls are ever before me."

When we get to the New Testament we find that the verbal proclamation of God's love pales in comparison to its demonstration. Who could have imagined giving a son—and not just any son!—in exchange for us! Words cannot begin to describe this incredible, saving act. Even these renowned words sound somehow insufficient: "For God so loved the world that he gave his one and only Son, that whoever believes in him shall not perish but have eternal life."[8]

John makes a stab at explaining this unthinkable event: "In the beginning was the Word, and the Word was with God, and the Word was God. He was with God in the beginning. Through him all things were made; without him nothing was made that has been made. In him was life, and that life was the light of men....

The Word became flesh and made his dwelling among us. We have seen his glory, the glory of the One and Only, who came from the Father, full of grace and truth."[9]

Even Wonderful Words Are Just Words

Yet as wonderful as the explanations are, they fall short. Unfortunately, having heard the story so often, we are deaf to its astounding music and somewhat ho-hum as to its effect. If only we could read the gospels as someone having never before heard the story, perhaps then we could feel the glorious collision, the thundering shock of human reason splattering against the irresistible onslaught of God.

Jesus' life and ministry collided with religious traditions and common sense. The human race had shifted so far off base that the truths by which God had intended us to live sounded almost bizarre. For example: " 'Love the Lord your God with all your heart and with all your soul and with all your strength and with all your mind'; and 'Love your neighbor as yourself.' "[10] and, "The greatest among you will be your servant." In explaining his mission, Jesus said, "For even the Son of Man did not come to be served, but to serve, and to give his life as a ransom for many."[11] When the words failed to penetrate, Jesus made it clear. "Having loved his own who were in the world, he now *showed them the full extent of his love.*" There follows the description of Christ washing his disciples' feet, after which Jesus says, "Do you understand what I have done for you?"[12]

What's the point? The point is that we serve a God who shows his love for us. If this transforming news is to help stop wars, stanch the flow of misery, and bring hope, we must show his love to others. "My command is this: Love each other as I have loved you."[13]

TO BE LIKE GOD WE MUST SHOW HIS LOVE TO OTHERS

Jesus didn't fit the mold prepared for him by Messianic prophets. During the four hundred years or so that elapsed between the events of the Old and New Testaments, Jewish writers produced prodigious amounts of apocryphal material, all anticipating the coming of the Messiah. The harsh persecution they suffered during these horrible years understandably affected their expectation of the Deliverer. By the time Jesus came, it was commonly believed that the Messiah would march his cleated armies through rivers of Roman blood, finally satisfying God's promise to the people of God (*i.e.*, the children of Abraham) that they would rule the nations of the world. How could any Messiah—even a divine figure—accomplish this without political clout? How could any Savior establish a Kingdom without armies and generals?

Both historical and contemporary history supported such a view. Egypt, that mighty empire with its pharaohs so hopelessly preoccupied with the afterlife, spent millions to erect mammoth tombs that were already ancient at the time of Christ. Egypt's chariots were legendary. Her armies ferocious. Monuments and memories of Egypt's forays and conquests lay scattered throughout Palestine.

Rome was preoccupied with conquest and power. Her armies tramped throughout the world, swallowing up nation after nation to push out the borders of her empire. Rome's emperors lusted after domination and control, some even aspiring to omnipotence. Every major city throughout Palestine had a Roman garrison, and Roman soldiers stood on every corner like the national guard.

Egypt treasured memories and monuments.

Rome prized power and politics.

Jesus cherished people.

It was unorthodox, to say the least. How could you build a kingdom by loving people? Kingdoms were built by slave labor. Could it be done with love?

Then, as now, we underestimate the power of love.

The Greatest Gift is Yourself

My parents-in-law, John and Florence Neal, pastored for more than fifty years in the Church of God on the West Coast. They were a team. Dad was a builder. A toolmaker by trade, he was also an excellent auto mechanic. While other people talked about blueprints, he was out pouring cement. He has left a remarkable legacy, and many pastors today can point to him as the one who inspired them to enter the ministry.

Mom was a supporter. A cook of considerable talent, she has single-handedly made more potato salad and homemade chicken and noodles than whole church-fulls of missionary societies. She directed children's programs, ran day cares, and threw in a few spaghetti dinners on the side.

Together they were formidable and wonderful. It seemed they would go on forever. Even in retirement Dad was clambering onto mobile homes to repair air-conditioning units, while Mom was inside praying and cooking.

In the early 1990s Parkinson's Disease threw a monkey wrench into Dad's lifestyle. His balance impaired, he stopped climbing on roofs. His once masterful stride was reduced to a shuffle, and he and his recliner spent more and more time together. But he could pray. And his eyes still twinkled when he told one of his old jokes just one more time.

Then Alzheimer's dealt a him a double whammy. Inside there somewhere is the man we love, but we cannot reach him any more. There are no more jokes. His eyes are glazed and unperceiving. How tragic that this man who cared all of his life for others now cannot care even for himself.

Mom is carrying the lion's share of the pain as these twin diseases render her husband immobile. As thousands in similar positions can testify, a quick death would be much easier to handle. Besides the overwhelming energy required of Mom to provide complete physical care, the emotional exhaustion is brutal. There are no moments of the day left unaffected. There is no time for naps. Sleep at night is constantly interrupted. No time to go to the store. No time even to have devotions. Karon and I live twenty-two hundred miles away. We have been able to help some, but Mom needs somebody to relieve her, now!

About a month ago, the phone rang in their Tucson mobile home. It was Harry, Mom's brother-in-law. He had for thirty or more years been married to Mom's sister, Peg, who died some years ago of cancer. Now remarried, he asked about Dad. Harry is no stranger to what Mom is going through. The last years of his care for Peg were heart-breaking as well as back-breaking. Mom has never complained, but Harry and his wife, Rosalee, picked up Mom's "Mayday!" cry with their sensitive hearts. They made this incredible offer: "Flo, I'll tell you what we're going to do. You pick the time and place. We'll come and spend two full weeks taking care of John. You go wherever you want and do whatever you please. We'll take complete responsibility for John's care. You won't have to worry about a thing."

Mom could scarcely believe it. Here was someone who not only understood, but wanted to do something about it. Only someone who had been drained by years-long care of an invalid could have known this was exactly what was needed. But——more important-ly—Harry and his wife decided to give the gift no one else could give. They gave themselves.

At the time of this writing, Mom is "on vacation." For the first several days she practically slept around the clock. She's done some reading. She's sending out the Christmas letters she had no time for earlier. She confessed on the telephone a couple of days ago, "I had no idea how bad I was!" Harry and Rosalee knew. They didn't only talk about love. They showed it.

DOES UNEXPRESSED LOVE EXIST?

In a real sense, love does not even exist until it is shared and shown. James argues, "What good is it, my brothers, if a man claims to have faith but has no deeds? Can such faith save him? Suppose a brother or sister is without clothes and daily food. If one of you says to him, 'Go, I wish you well; keep warm and well fed,' but does nothing about his physical needs, what good is it?"[14] None of us needs any more pressure or guilt, to be sure. Yet there is truth in the old saying, "Hell is paved with good intentions."[15] We must put feet on our love. To do so brings positive, practical heal-ing.

How Will You Know Unless I Tell You?

A single schoolteacher moved to a new community. I'll call her Elaine.[16] Of course, it wasn't new except for her. As a matter of fact, it was a well established, older community in a small town in the midwest. Everyone knew each other, except for Elaine. Rituals and traditions were well established, except Elaine didn't know what they were. It wasn't that anyone intended to be unfriendly, but no one ever phoned to say hello. People kept to themselves, with no one making much effort to include Elaine. She attended the small community church spasmodically. You know how it is. People would nod and smile. But after the service they would go to each other's homes, or perhaps they would just go home by themselves. Elaine was simply and excruciatingly alone.

Winter came. It so happened that an old illness flared up which required a doctor's care. It wasn't serious, and Elaine didn't talk about it much, except perhaps to make a comment in the teacher's lounge, or to arrange with the principal for the two weeks' time off the convalescence from surgery would require. By this time she had determined that even though her fellow teachers kept mostly to themselves, she would make more of an effort to be friendly. She would stop by different classrooms on the way to her room each morning, smile brightly and offer a cheerful, "Good morning." The response was underwhelming, to say the least.

The day for her surgery arrived. It was raining. She moved slowly through her small house, thinking how like the rain her life had become: cold, gray, cheerless. Her bag packed, she prepared a small lunch of tomato soup and toast. Just as she was sitting down, she heard the mail carrier on the front porch. She walked into the front hallway, knowing there would be the usual: "Occupant" letters, advertisements from computers whose operators misspelled her name, bills, perhaps a Walter Drake catalog. Sorting through the mail at the table, she spotted a sunny yellow envelope. She did not recognize either the handwriting or the return address. Puzzled, she slit it open. She did notice that her name was spelled correctly.

On brightly colored note paper she read, "Dear Elaine, I have been thinking about you lately. I know your move here has not been easy. We are such a fuddy-duddy group and keep to ourselves. We don't mean to be standoffish.

"Everybody likes you at school. You will never know how much it means to hear your cheerful, 'Good morning,' every day. I look forward to it each morning.

"I just found out that you will be having minor surgery and will be out for a couple of weeks. When I heard it, my first thought was, How will I get through the day without Elaine's 'Good morning'? And while I sat, feeling sorry for myself, I suddenly realized that you had no idea how much you mean to me. How could you? You didn't know that I think you're a competent, caring teacher. You didn't know that I'm glad you moved to town. You didn't know that I'll miss you. You didn't know: I'll be praying for you.

"Today I wanted you to know that I'll miss you. How will you know unless I tell you?"

Elaine sat, her soup untouched. Tears welled up in her eyes. "Thank you, God," she whispered. "Thank you so much."

The love existed in the heart of the one who wrote the note before the note was written. Elaine only received its transfusion of warmth when someone showed it.

TO WHOM MUST WE SHOW OUR LOVE?

Our personal relationship to God is the peg on which our entire Christian experience hangs. Newly converted Christians often exhibit an intense awareness of God in their lives. They rejoice almost hourly in God's forgiveness. They return repeatedly, like children rushing again and again into the ocean's waves, to exult in God's love.

In time, the daily routines of life seep into the once impassioned relationship. Like a slowly rising river the cold, wet realities of tradition and habit extinguish the glowing coals that once warmed the heart. Newspapers and television slowly usurp the time once dedicated to reading the Bible. Impossible schedules and the hectic pace of life strangle our intentions to pray.

Has this happened to you?

We First Show Our Love for God
Through Cultivating the "Light Within"

At the urging of Irene Caldwell years ago, I bought and read several classics of Christian devotional literature.[17] All have influenced my thinking, but perhaps none so deeply as A *Testament of Devotion* by Thomas R. Kelly.[18] "Deep within us all," he writes, "there is an amazing inner sanctuary of the soul, a holy place, a Divine Center, a speaking Voice, to which we may continuously return. Eternity is at our hearts, pressing upon our time-torn lives, warming us with intimations of an astounding destiny, calling us home unto Itself. Yielding to these persuasions, gladly committing ourselves in body and soul, utterly and completely, to the Light Within, is the beginning of true life."[19]

Mr. Kelly is not in any way referring to the New Age teachings so prevalent today, which imply that each of us is in charge of his or her own destiny. He explains, "In this humanistic age we suppose man is the initiator and God is the responder. But the Living Christ within us is the initiator and we are the responders. God the Lover, the accuser, the revealer of light and darkness presses within us. 'Behold I stand at the door and knock.' And all our apparent initiative is already a response, a testimonial to His secret presence and working within us."[20]

In the following paragraph Kelly describes a fervent experience, the reading of which makes me ache to know Christ better.

> The basic response of the soul to Light is internal adoration and joy, thanksgiving and worship, self-surrender and listening. The secret places of the heart cease to be our noisy workshop. They become a holy sanctuary of adoration and of self-oblation, where we are kept in perfect peace, if our minds be stayed on Him who has found us in the inward springs of our life. And in brief intervals of overpowering visitation we are able to carry the sanctuary frame of mind out into the world, into its turmoil and its fitfulness, and in a hyperaesthesia of the soul we see all mankind tinged with deeper shadows, and touched with Galilean glories. Powerfully are the springs of our will moved to an abandon of singing love toward God; powerfully are we moved to a new and overcoming love toward time-blinded men and all creation. In this Center of Creation all things are ours, and we are Christ's and Christ is God's. We are owned men, ready to run and not be weary and to walk and not faint.[21]

These words flow from the heart of a man who walked with God. He grasped that first we must love God before we can love others. Do you have a secret place in your heart that is a holy sanctuary of adoration? Do you there find Christ's perfect peace? Does his presence renew the inward springs of your life? Where are the Christians today who "carry the sanctuary frame of mind out into the world"? Where are those "powerfully moved to an overcoming love toward time-blinded men"? When was the last time your heart was quickened to singing because God himself is with you? Are we "owned men [and women]"? Who is it, exactly, who owns us?

Second, We Show Our Love for God through Obedience.

A. W. Tozer writes,

> The moment we make up our minds that we are going on with this determination to exalt God over all we step out of the world's parade. We shall find ourselves out of adjustment to the ways of the world and increasingly so as we make progress....
>
> Our break with the world will be the direct outcome of our changed relation to God. For the world of fallen men does not honor God. Millions call themselves by His Name, it is true, and pay some token respect to Him, but a simple test will show how little He is really honored among them. Let the average man be put to the proof on the questions of who is above, and his true position will be exposed. Let him be forced into making a choice between God and money, between God and men, between God and personal ambition, God and self, God and human love, and God will take second place every time. Those other things will be exalted above. However the man may protest, the proof is in the choices he makes day after day throughout his life.[22]

Dr. Tozer is saying that our love for God is hollow and ineffectual if it is not shown. Words are empty if not backed by deeds. Is it possible to love God and not show it? Can we show our love to God in ways other than obedience? One can almost hear the pain and exasperation in Christ's voice as he pleads, "Why do you call me, 'Lord, Lord,' and do not do what I say?"[23]

Tozer continues with this eloquent appeal: "Let no one imagine that he will lose anything of human dignity by this voluntary sell-out of his all to his God. He does not by this degrade himself as a man; rather he finds his right place of high honor as one made in the image of his Creator....

"Anyone who might feel reluctant to surrender his will to the will of another should remember Jesus' words, 'Whosoever committeth sin is the servant of sin.' ... The sinner prides himself on his independence, completely overlooking the fact that he is the weak slave of the sins that rule his members. The man who surrenders to Christ exchanges a cruel slave driver for a kind and gentle Master whose yoke is easy and whose burden is light."[24]

How Can We Show Our Love to Others?

Practical. God is always practical. People cannot appreciate what they do not understand. The most enraptured inner experience with God will bless no one but you unless it comes out in practical ways.

Jesus came enjoying life.[25] He identified with ordinary people, and helped them in ordinary ways they could understand. His death and resurrection, above all, were eminently practical. His was not an ethereal encouragement that sounded nice but rang hollow. He didn't come only to preach sermons. The genius of Christ's encouragement to the world lies in his practical, easily understood acts of kindness and selflessness. There are no strings attached, and no hidden agendas. We have so much to learn.

Vicarious Death

In his book, *Written in Blood*, Robert Coleman tells the story of a little boy whose sister needed a blood transfusion. The doctor explained that she had the same disease the boy had recovered from two years earlier. Her only chance for recovery was a transfusion from someone who had previously conquered the disease. Since the two children had the same rare blood type, the boy was the ideal donor.

"Would you give your blood to Mary?" the doctor asked.

Johnny hesitated. His lower lip started to tremble. Then he smiled and said, "Sure, for my sister."

Soon the two children were wheeled into the hospital room—Mary, pale and thin; Johnny, robust and healthy. Neither spoke, but when their eyes met, Johnny grinned.

As the nurse inserted the needle into his arm, Johnny's smile faded. He watched the blood flow through the tube.

With the ordeal almost over, his voice, slightly shaky, broke the silence, "Doctor, when do I die?"

Only then did the doctor realize why Johnny had hesitated, why his lip had trembled when he'd agreed to donate his blood. He'd thought giving his blood to his sister meant giving up his life. In that brief moment, he'd made his great decision.

Johnny, fortunately, didn't have to die to save his sister. Each of us, however, has a condition more serious than Mary's, and it required Jesus to give not just his blood but his life.[26]

Practical. Always Practical.

Encouragement. How does it come? John and Gwen Johnson, missionaries to Egypt, shared two great examples in their January 1994 newsletter.

The first has to do with a new church building going up in Shoubra, a poor section of Cairo. Money has come from many places to help fund this expensive but critical project. Some of us may have helped. In December of 1993 help arrived from an unexpected quarter: a small church in Japan. Missionary Bernie Barton brought greetings during a December service of the Shoubra congregation. After sharing about Christians in Japan, Bernie presented sixteen hundred dollars to help construct the building in Cairo. The women of the church had a bake sale in the fall to raise five hundred dollars of the money. (What a bake sale!)

In addition, half of the Christmas Eve service offering, taken the night before Bernie boarded the plane for Egypt, was given for the Shoubra Project!

The Johnsons write, "What a wonderful picture of community. A small church in Japan works together and gathers gifts to present to other Christians that they will never meet, in order that the second group might be able to have a suitable place to worship. When Brother Mounir (the pastor at Shoubra) returned to the pulpit to speak he said the contractor had asked him for some more money to pay certain bills the day before, 'Now I have something to give him,' he said."

The second took place at a geriatric center run by the Egyptian Catholic Church. The Johnsons, Downeys, and about fifteen others from the Cairo Christian Fellowship had gone caroling. They sang in the halls and visited with patients, one of whom was a teacher years ago to many of those who were caroling.

At one point, Jonni, the Johnson's young daughter, looked up and asked if they could go because she was bored. Her father reminded her of the joy that they were bringing. Then he asked, "Did you know that we are visiting Jesus?" He explained what Jesus relates in Matthew 25 about visiting the sick, "I tell you the truth, whatever you did for the least of these you did it to me." Jonni never said another word about being bored the entire evening.

ENCOURAGEMENT TRANSFORMS LIFE

"Warmth, warmth, and more warmth. For the world is dying of cold, and not of darkness. It is not the night that kills, but the frost." These arresting words come from Miguel de Unamuno, a Spanish novelist of the last century. He graphically portrays today's society, filled with people who are so angry they will open fire on complete strangers. Human compassion is in such short supply. Loneliness engulfs our big cities, isolating millions from meaningful relationships with the other millions who jostle them on the sidewalks and honk at them on the freeways.

And what will warmth do? Change the world, that's what! Leo Buscaglia gave the students of his Love Class an assignment to share themselves, without expectation of reward. He writes,

I went with one of my students, Joel, to a nursing home not far from USC. A number of aged people were lying in beds in old cotton gowns, staring at the ceiling. Joel looked around then asked, "What'll I do?" I said, "You see that woman over there? Go say hello."

He went over and said, "Uh, hello."

She looked at him suspiciously for a minute, "Are you a relative?"

"No."

"Good! Sit down, young man."

Oh, the things she told him! This woman knew so much about love, pain, suffering. Even about approaching death, with which she had to make some kind of peace. But no one had cared about listening—until Joel. He started visiting her once a week. Soon, that day began to be known as "Joel's Day." He would come and all the old people would gather.

Then the elderly woman asked her daughter to bring her in a glamorous dressing gown. When Joel came for his visit, he found her sitting up in bed in a beautiful satin gown, her hair done up stylishly. She hadn't had her hair fixed in ages: why have your hair done if nobody really sees you? Before long, others in the ward were dressing up for Joel.[27]

"And let us consider how we may spur one another on toward love and good deeds…. But let us encourage one another—and all the more as you see the Day approaching."[28]

QUESTIONS FOR DISCUSSION

1. The author states, "To live with the purpose of encouraging others is one of the hardest lessons for us to learn." Do you agree with this? Why or why not?

2. Discuss Bob Benson's concept, "You made me what I am." Is this consistent with the scriptural teaching that each of us is accountable for our own lives? (Ezek. 18:20, Rom. 14:12).

3. What are the barriers in local churches that keep people from understanding how much God loves them?

4. What's the difference in the statements that "God loves the unlovable" and "In everyone he sees something lovable"?

5. How do the scriptures and promises given to God's chosen people in the Psalms relate to Christians today? Can we confidently assume they apply to us? What about the gift of Jesus Christ to the world?

6. What are some specific ways you know God shows his love for you, personally?

7. Do you agree with this statement: "In a real sense, love does not even exist until it is shared and shown"?

8. Discuss the idea of showing our love to God. In what ways do you let God know you love him?

9. What things keep us from giving ourselves to others in love? Specifically, how will you adjust your lifestyle to live a life of encouragement?

NOTES

1. David Dunn, *Try Giving Yourself Away* (Englewood Cliffs, NJ: Prentice-Hall, Inc, 1947, 1956), ix.

2. Leo Buscaglia, "The Girl in the Fifth Row, " *Reader's Digest,* (February 1984), 33–34.

3. John 15:13 (NIV)

4. Matthew 25:34–40 (RSV)

5. Bob Benson, *Something's Going on Here,* (Nashville: Impact Books, 1977), 79–80.

6. For 125 delightful and unorthodox glimpses of the Bible's people, read Frederick Buechner, *Peculiar Treasures* (San Francisco: Harper & Row, 1979). These phrases are take from the book's fly-leaf.

7. Read in the newsletter of the Hercules Community Church of God, Clearwater, Florida (Sept. 19, 1983).

8. John 3:16

9. John 1:1–4, 14

10. Luke 10:27

11. Mark 10:45

12. John 13:1, 12

13. John 15:12

14. James 2:14–16

15. English proverb

16. I could not locate the source of this true, heartwarming story.

17. Some of these are *The Imitation of Christ,* Thomas a Kempis; *Pilgrim's Progress,* John Bunyan; *A Testament of Devotion,* Thomas R. Kelly; *The Practice of the Presence of God,* Brother Lawrence; *The Christian's Secret of a Happy Life* and *The God of All Comfort,* Hannah Whitall Smith; and *My Utmost for His Highest,* Oswald Chambers.

18. Thomas R. Kelly, *A Testament of Devotion* (New York: Harper & Row, 1941).

19. Kelly 29

20. p. 30
21. p. 30
22. A. W. Tozer, *The Pursuit of God*, (Harrisburg, Pa: Christian Publications, Inc.), 102–103.
23. Luke 6:46
24. Tozer 104
25. Luke 7:34
26. Thomas Lindberg, "To Illustrate ..." *Leadership* (Winter, 1984), 54.
27. Buscaglia 38
28. Hebrews 10:24–25

5

God Is Speaking: Strengthen the Family

Hebrews 12:5–13

WHY SHOULD WE STRENGTHEN THE FAMILY?

The Biblical Pattern

Scripture overflows with references to the family unit. Is this by design or by accident? Well, it's obvious that the cultural environment of the period is a major influence.[1] While here and there in the Old Testament we catch fleeting glimpses of the idea women are to be highly valued and respected as leaders, and while Jesus, Luke, and Paul break further ground toward this ideal, we must admit the overwhelming feeling throughout the Bible is that men rule the home, the country, and the world, and women bear children and do what they're told.[2] If this heavy-handed cultural predisposition were the only reason for strong family emphasis in scripture, we might somewhat discount the importance of the family unit by reasoning that customs change.

The family unit, however, stands at the core of Christian teaching. Even in the age of the patriarchs the family unit was treated with high regard. Our concepts of theology spring from such thinking. Jesus was born into a family. He grew up under the care of a mother and father like everybody else. This cannot have been a coincidence. God's Son could as easily have entered the world as an adult and thus missed the agonies of sibling rivalry and adolescence. But there is such value in childhood and in growing up in a caring home that God predetermined his own Son should experience it. Repeatedly the scriptures compare God to our Father. Jesus said that we were his own brothers and sisters.[3] Why so? Families are the foundational unit of society. Respect for God and an understanding of his authority were to be learned in the home.[4] The Hebrew writer assumes family experience when he elevates the value of discipline in the home.[5] In fact, he goes so far as to say that undisciplined children are illegitimate and not "true sons."

The family unit is built on marriage, and no view of marriage is higher than that of the Bible. The marriage bed is to be kept inviolate.[6] Adultery was punishable by death.[7] The prophets who bemoaned Israel's unfaithfulness to Jehovah used images of adultery as the ultimate comparison to jolt people into a realization of how serious their idolatry had become.[8] While adultery symbolizes idolatry, weddings and marriage symbolize God's joy and pleasure with the righteous.[9] Paul uses marriage to illustrate the pure, holy love God feels toward the church.[10] And John, writer of Revelation, sees the grand culmination of all history as a glorious wedding feast celebrating the union of God and his chosen people.[11]

The Contemporary Pattern

Respect for marriage and the home in America are at a new low. The traditional family unit is disintegrating. The 1994 Los Angeles earthquake was a ripple compared to the incredible disasters mangling our homes today. Never before in history have traditional cultural patterns been so radically altered. Families are succumbing to stress, overstimulation, and selfishness. On the fringes of this unparalleled breakup stand the liberals and media darlings who spout absurdities like a family unit can as well consist of two women with children, two men with children, or two or more unmarried adults living together with children. In the middle of this momentous social upheaval stand the ordinary people—many of them Christians—who have lost any sense of moral direction. Unable to see any compelling reasons to postpone gratification or honor marriage, they are abandoning their spouses and children in record numbers.

Hallmark cards, after extensive and well-funded market research, has created several lines of greetings cards aimed at the swelling tide of people caught in the divorce crunch. "Think of your former marriage as a record album," says one Hallmark greeting card. "It was full of music—both happy and sad. But what's important now is—YOU! The recently released HOT, NEW SINGLE! You're going to be at the TOP OF THE CHARTS!" Another card carries this message: "Getting divorced can be very healthy! Watch how it improves your circulation!"[12]

Ms. Barbara Dafoe cites a growing flood of books and magazines aimed at the swelling audience of the divorced. According to one study, eighty percent of divorced women and fifty percent of divorced men say they are better off out of their marriages.[13] The dominant view in popular culture is that these changes in family structure are for the most part positive. Critics of popular culture like Dr. James Dobson are blasted as doomsayers and antiquated fundamentalists who are unwilling to accept the new facts of life.

Children Pay the Price

But the evidence is in. Divorce is transforming the lives of American children. Over the past two and one-half decades Americans have been conducting a vast natural experiment in family life. The results are clear. Only fifty percent of children will grow up with both biological parents. Each year more than a million children experience family breakup: about as many are born out of wedlock. Family disruptions have grown. Child well-being has declined. Teen suicide rates have almost tripled since World War II. Juvenile crime has increased and become more violent. School performance has been poor.[14]

Although many therapists, lawyers, and parents do not welcome the news, studies show that children of divorce suffer depression and maladjustment into adulthood five, ten, and fifteen years after the fact. Many struggle to establish strong love relationships of their own. They are at greater risk for precocious sexuality, teenage marriage, teen pregnancy, and divorce. Educational attainment is significantly lower. Fathers, especially, suffer maladjustment in their relationships with children from former marriages. Even mother-child relationships deteriorate. Given such a dramatic impact on children's lives, one might expect today's high divorce rate to be viewed more widely as a national crisis.[15]

START BY STRENGTHENING MARRIAGE

A couple of paragraphs above I mentioned the L.A. earthquake of 1994. The following observation may seem so obvious that it's insulting, but bear with me. The freeways and buildings that survived invariably (a) had a solid foundation (b) were well constructed, and (c) were well maintained. I watched a city engineer being interviewed shortly after several freeway overpasses collapsed. His comment was that the fallen structures had been targeted for strengthening later in the year, but the earthquake came too soon.

Any family that is to survive the earthquakes of social upheaval that are now devastating American society must also be well founded, well constructed, and well maintained. And no family is stronger than the marriage that supports it. How can we build strong marriages?

BEDROCK SCRIPTURE FOR MARRIAGE

Scripture provides the most enduring guidance for husbands and wives who want to build a strong marriage and family. American life in the 1990s gives eloquent if somber testimony to the fact that the farther from Christian principles our society moves, the less stable our marriages and families become. It might be argued that many strong marriages have no doubt existed without any conscious Christian commitment on the part of the spouses. My response to this is two-fold: (1) surely the husbands and wives of those marriages are unconsciously following biblical principles, and (2) each of those marriages would have been improved if God's principles had been knowingly followed.

THE "BEFORE MARRIAGE" CHECKLIST

1. Marriage Is for Keeps.

A lively discussion between Jesus and the Pharisees is reported in Mark 10:1–12. In response to their argument that even Moses had authorized divorce, Jesus explained, "It was because your hearts were hard that Moses wrote you this law." Christ then outlines God's original intent for marriage: "At the beginning of creation God 'made them male and female.' For this reason a man will leave his father and mother and be united to his wife, and the two will become one flesh. So they are no longer two, but one. Therefore what God has joined together, let man not separate." God intends for each husband and wife to remain faithful for life. Marriage is not a convenient relationship to try on for size and then discard if it doesn't meet one's expectations.

A young woman who worked near my wife was preparing for her wedding day. As she left the office the morning of the ceremony, a well-wisher commented, "You don't seem very happy to be getting married." The bride-to-be tossed her answer over her shoulder on the way out the door, "Oh, I give it six months." With such a cavalier attitude marriage has no hope of surviving.

2. Love Alone Is Not Enough

Because marriage is for keeps, "love alone" is not a satisfactory reason to say "I do." To live with one person all your life takes more than the popular variety of physical infatuation that propels so many people to the marriage altar these days. It also takes determination and grace. Some wag quipped, "Many a man in love with a dimple has made the mistake of marrying the whole girl." This zinger hits the nail on the head: you get a lot more than looks when you tie the knot.

3. What do you get?

You marry one person, but you actually tie the knot with a whole family. Even if you live miles from your in-laws and other relatives, you get the family in your spouse. Each of us brings a complex mixture of our families and environment to marriage. From how children are disciplined to what's an appropriate breakfast on Saturday morning, years of traditions and expectations are joined at the altar when you say "I do." Current psychological research supports the view that we are in fact indelibly imprinted with our families' entire methods of operation.[16] In other words, there's more than quaint folklore in the phrase, "Take a good look at your fiancée's mother. That's what your wife will be like in thirty years." (Or make it your fiancé's father.) Throughout life husbands and wives discover new things about each other. Marriage is a wedding gift that you unwrap over fifty years bit by bit. Quite often you find something you did not expect.

4. Life Is a Risk

When we marry we inherit an uncertain future. Recently a young husband and wife were involved in a bicycle accident. Unbelievably, the woman sustained injuries so severe that one of her legs had to be amputated six inches above the knee. If the wife's athletic figure were the basis of her husband's love for her, this marriage is in trouble. When trouble comes, infatuation fizzles. And life is full of trouble! Financial crises, imperfect children, unexpected job losses, in-law quarrels, crippling illnesses: every such predicament taxes even the best marriage. Only the committed and determined will stay true.

Because marriage is for keeps, we must approach it cautiously. Jesus told a parable about a man who started to build a tower. He rushed into it and laid the foundation, but soon ran out of funds. The half-built structure remained unfinished, and the man was ridiculed for his lack of foresight and common sense.[17] Some people spend more time buying a car than they do in selecting a life's companion!

When our children began casting in matrimonial waters, we

gave them these pieces of advice (I'm sure they'd say we never stopped giving them advice!): Become good friends first. Get to know each other. Ask about values, religious commitment, and life goals. Then if love comes, you have a chance. Amos asked "Do two walk together unless they have agreed to do so?"[18]

In the witty Broadway musical, *Candide,* the hero and heroine are preparing for marriage. Each is very much in love with the idea of marriage, but their expectations couldn't be farther apart!

They sing:

He: Soon, when we can afford it, we'll build a modest little farm.
She: We'll buy a yacht and live aboard it, rolling in luxury and stylish charm.
He: Cows and chickens!
She: Social whirls!
He: Peas and cabbage!
She: Ropes of pearls!
He: Soon there'll be little ones beside us, we'll have a sweet Westphalian home.
She: Somehow we'll grow as rich as Midas! We'll live in Paris when we're not in Rome!
He: Smiling Babies!
She: Marble halls!
He: Sunlit Picnics!
She: Costume balls!
She: I'll have robes of silk and satin, I'll have everything I can desire.
He: We'll spend the evenings growing fat and dream dreams beside the fire.
She: Glowing rubies!
He: Glowing logs!
She: Faithful servants!
He: Faithful dogs!
She: We'll round the world enjoying highlights, all will be pink champagne and gold!
He: We'll lead a rustic and a shy life, leading the pigs and sweetly growing old.

She: Breast of peacock!
He: Apple pie!
She: I love marriage!
He: So do I!
Together: O happy pair! O happy we! It's very rare how we
    agree![19]

5. Love Won't Cover Up Who You Are

You make the marriage. The marriage doesn't make you. No marriage can be stronger than the weakest personality trait you bring to it. Success in marriage consists not only in finding the right mate, but in being the right mate.

We were at a friend's home for dinner. The roast beef and mashed potatoes were delicious, and now it was time for dessert. Our hostess set large pieces of chocolate cake before us, slathered with thick white icing. As we began to eat I thought, "Something's not quite right with this cake." I couldn't put my finger on it, but there was a definite under taste with which I was unfamiliar. Halfway through desert, she exclaimed, "Did you figure out what the secret ingredient is in the cake? Mayonnaise!" I could barely finish. The white icing, especially, suddenly tasted like I was licking the spatula straight from the mayonnaise jar. I'm not much of a connoisseur, but there's one thing I'll say: mayonnaise wasn't meant to go in cakes. No matter what you add to it, it will always taste like mayonnaise. (Apologies to those who really do like Miracle Whip cake.)

Marriage is a lot more complex and wonderful than a chocolate cake, yet it's true that each partner brings distinctive flavors to the marriage. No amount of education or dress will ever conceal the basic flavor of each partner's personality. Make sure you like the taste before you put it in the cake.

6. Do Not Mismate

"Do not be yoked together with unbelievers. For what do righteousness and wickedness have in common? Or what fellowship can light have with darkness? What harmony is there between Christ

100

and [idols]? What does a believer have in common with an unbeliever?"[20]

It has always been a challenge for Christian parents to convince their offspring that Paul knew what he was talking about. Quite frankly, a lot of Christians take his advice with a grain of salt. America of the 1990s has become more and more tolerant of divergent religious beliefs. In many ways this is wonderful, for we need to accept people where they are. But we must not indiscriminately form intimate relationships with those who do not love God, or we may end up marrying them, and that's trouble. Why is this a problem?

Mismating Jeopardizes Your Own Christian Experience

Let's start with dating. The whole world of where to go and what to do will be colored by the morality and ideals of those who date each other. A young man or woman who is eager to please and romantically involved will find it increasingly difficult to hold standards his or her companion does not share. The longer the relationship lasts, the deeper the crisis grows. It is a rare adolescent who will hold the line under this kind of pressure. Once any standard is relaxed, the floodgates open. Further restraint is exceedingly difficult.

It is very common for young Christian women to approach believer/unbeliever dating with missionary zeal. They plan to convert their boyfriends! Many actually believe God is arranging their romance in order to evangelize the young men of their dreams. I personally doubt God leads this way. It is too dangerous. Often the young unbeliever will engineer a "religious experience" to win his or her love. On the other hand, if your true love won't change in order to win your hand, why will he or she change once they've got you?

When such relationships lead to marriage, they begin on a cracked foundation. Even if the Christian partner managed to hold his or her standards before the wedding, to do so now is more difficult. What about church attendance? Tithing? When children come, what will be taught them, and by which parent? How will they know which parent is speaking the truth?

In order to keep peace in the family, personal Christian convictions are often sacrificed. When one is in love, and God seems to be dividing husband and wife, who wouldn't favor dismissing God to rid themselves of constant tension within the home? These difficult questions persist through the years, issues that pit being faithful to a spouse versus being faithful to God. Even if the Christian spouse manages to maintain a dynamic walk with God, it will be an uphill battle all the way. Marriage has enough battles to be fought without fighting about things like where God fits into the home.

Mismating Weakens the Marriage Bond

For a Christian to marry an unbeliever is like buying a new car that's a lemon. Have you ever owned a car like that? I did. It was a beautiful car from every appearance, but it had one fatal flaw: the engine would die unexpectedly and without warning, often in the middle of intersections or when pulling into oncoming traffic. Time after time we had it repaired. It just couldn't be fixed. So we junked it.

But marriages aren't cars to be junked. Responsible Christian adults will try repeatedly over the years to repair what should never have been started in the first place: a marriage between a Christian and a non-Christian. Such marriages often do not survive. If they do, it will be at great sacrifice.

Remember that I'm talking now about God's principles to be considered before marriage. If you are already committed to such a marriage, God will surely help you and support you.

GOD'S "AFTER THE WEDDING" PRINCIPLES

God's marriage principles can be summed up in Paul's admonition, "Submit to one another out of reverence for Christ."[21] Paul gives us the most beautiful and practical advice for marriage found in Scripture. In Ephesians 5:21–28 he prescribes specific attitudes for both spouses: submission and love. In 1 Corinthians 13 he describes the kind of love he is talking about when he says to "love as Christ loved the church."

"Love is patient, love is kind. It does not envy, it does not boast, it is not proud. It is not rude, it is not self-seeking, it is not easily angered, it keeps no record of wrongs. Love does not delight in evil but rejoices with the truth. It always protects, always trusts, always hopes, always perseveres. Love never fails."[22]

At the risk of reducing these sublime concepts, let me sketch some of their practical applications:

Give, Give, Give

A woman came to her husband with a list of his faults. His reply, "I know all about those. That's what kept me from getting a better woman!" Wouldn't you say this couple had a negative focus?

God is the first giver. God's style is to give lavishly and extravagantly. As marriage partners we must get beyond the I'll-do-this-if-you'll-do-that mentality. Love does not barter. Paul said love is not self-seeking. My attitude as a husband must be, "How can I love you today?" "How can I serve you today?" "How can I make you look good today?"

We must take the initiative to give. Do the dishes. Make the bed. Stay up late to play Monopoly. Think, "How would I like to be treated?" and treat your spouse that way. Never let a day pass without saying at least one complimentary thing to each other. Note the good. Overlook the bad.

Talk, Talk, Talk, But Don't Nag, Nag, Nag!

In order to "rejoice in the truth,"[23] we must communicate with each other. Watching television together is really not communicating. How can I compete with *Wheel of Fortune* or twenty-four-hour news? If you love me you'll listen to me. What's more, you'll tell me what you're thinking and how you feel. One young man who had come to me for marital counseling confessed that he and his wife were not communicating. When I suggested they set aside a special time each day to talk, he said, "That's not my nature." It was an excuse to avoid making an effort to love. Love communicates.

As we communicate, love will flavor our attitudes and our

choice of words. One marriage counselor I know advises, "Never yell at each other unless the house is on fire." Love will avoid trigger words like "always" and "never." Love will not attack or respond in anger with hurtful phrases. Good business management teaches that we must focus on the issue, and not on the person. This makes sense in marriage, too.

Expect Imperfection

If love "keeps no record of wrongs,"[24] Paul is assuming someone isn't perfect. To enter marriage with the intent to make over your husband or wife is foolish. Yet how many of us insist, day after day, that our mate change a habit or hobby to please us? My poor wife has for many years had to put up with a compulsive husband. What's worse, for many years I felt my passion to always put everything away (immediately!) was a superior quality! While she lovingly endured, I even harped at her to become like me. Years ago she must have heard the gentleman who said, "Every day, forgive your spouse from the bottom of your heart." For what? For being who they are. While you're at it, ask God to help you treasure them as they are.

Allow space between you. A perfect marriage does not mean you must always be together and do everything together. When couples light the unity candle at their weddings, I encourage them to leave each of their own candles burning. We each remain a person with hopes, joys, and personalities of our own. Good marriages will treasure these differences. Such space between us is like the space between the pillars that support a temple. If the pillars were too close to each other, the building would collapse.

Do Not Lie

Love "rejoices in the truth."[25] No organization can survive without trust; not even hell, according to Jesus.[26] We may not agree, my wife and I, but we know we have not withheld the truth from each other. We can face the world and anything it can throw at us because we trust each other. One lie will erode that faith. Honesty will strengthen it.

Paul Tournier writes about the healing power of confession.

> One time God directed me to share with a patient something that to me seemed so trivial—indeed faintly embarrassing—that only years of learning to trust him made me do it.
> This particular man had been coming to see me for weeks without ever getting down to what was really bothering him. One morning he asked me, "How do you use the quiet time you speak of in your books?"
> Suspecting that he was not really interested but just seeking again to avoid some subject that frightened him, I said "Let's not talk about it. Let's try it." We closed our eyes, and I prayed earnestly that he might have a real experience with God. How faith building it would be if he would give us both some inspiring message!
> But instead of inspiration all I seemed able to think about was the bills that were due this month. I've got to sit down tonight, I thought, and go over the household accounts with my wife. This would never do! I should have been setting an example of prayer, not fretting over money!
> Then came the unmistakable directive: Confess to this man what you've been thinking about.
> Well, I wrestled as I always did; I finally got it out.
> He looked startled. "That is my problem!" he cried, "I must lie to my wife about money every day because I have a secret life. How did you know?"
> With the truth at last out in the open, we were able to face his problems together. But it might not have happened if I had tried to hide behind the facade of "spiritual" mentor. If, in fact, I had declined to share my very fallible self.
> But I have found that it is not when we are most lofty-minded but when we are most human that we come closest to God.[27]

Confessing one's fears and faults to a loving spouse brings support and strength. It goes without saying that such secrets will always be kept in the strictest confidence.

Draw Close to God

Have you heard about the "heavenly triangle"? I always share this simple diagram as part of the last session of premarital counseling. To draw this triangle, mark three black dots on a piece of paper, with two dots at the bottom, and the third above. The bottom dots depict the husband and wife. The upper dot represents God. Join a line from one of the lower dots to the upper dot. Repeat with the other dot to complete the triangle. Note this: as each partner draws closer to God, he or she also nears his (her) marriage partner.

Drawing close to God keeps your perspectives straight. God strengthens against temptation and reminds of promises made. God will help you take the initiative for spiritual growth in your home and marriage.

Leo Tolstoy wrote, "The goal of our life should not be to find joy in marriage, but to bring more love and truth into the world. We marry to assist each other in this task. The most selfish and hateful life of all is that of two beings who unite in order to enjoy life. The highest calling is that of the man who has dedicated his life to serving God and doing good, and who unites with a woman in order to further that purpose."

BEDROCK SCRIPTURE FOR PARENTING

Supposing husband and wife are Christians who have a strong marriage, what biblical direction is there for building a strong family? An example of such teachings is listed by the *Thompson Chain Reference Bible*. Here is an excellent outline of scriptural duties for parents, and I urge you to study these scriptures:

1. To teach (Deuteronomy. 6:7, 20, 21:19)
2. To train (Proverbs 22:6, Isaiah 38:19, Lamentations 2:19)
3. To provide for (2 Corinthians 12:14)

4. To nurture (Ephesians 6:4; Colossians 3:21)
5. To control (1 Timothy 3:4, 12)
6. To love (Titus 2:4)[28]

Of course the Bible offers a great deal more than these few specific injunctions for parents and family life. The Bible also provides us with both general guidelines (throughout) as well as Christ's teaching. In other words, scriptures like 1 Corinthians 13, to which we referred earlier regarding marriage, also teach us about family relationships. Jesus told one parable in particular that portrays the kind of family life God intends for us. Here is the story in an updated setting. The truths are the same.

THE PRODIGAL, RETOLD[29]

There was a man who had two sons. The younger, named Sam, said to his father, "Dad, I know you're planning to split your estate between me and Roger when you die. I've been thinking, Why should I wait until then to get the benefit of that capital? If you could see your way clear to let me have the money now, I could invest it and go into business as I've always dreamed. That way I'll be ahead of the game and get out of your hair here on the ranch. You know I'll never be a rancher like Roger."

His father was somewhat taken aback at Sam's forthright request. But the more he thought it over the more sense it made to him. Sam was a people-person. He was always having friends over for a pool party or barbecue. But Roger was a loner who never wanted to leave the ranch. He loved to ride off into the late afternoons, not coming back until nightfall.

Sam was elated the morning his father called him into his office and presented him with his portfolio. There were stocks, bonds, and a cashier's check for a substantial amount of money. "If you invest this wisely, Sam, you will be well off. In a few years you will have sufficient capital to start your own public relations firm without having to touch the principal investment. I think you'll do well."

Roger was shocked and at first angered at Sam's departure. But then he had the ranch, and that's what he always wanted.

Actually, he was somewhat relieved that Sam was leaving. Their relationship had always been limited—they were so different from each other.

Sam moved to the coast to the big city where he had some promising contacts. When he called now and then, he sounded quite optimistic. Roger and his father settled into the routines of ranch life without Sam. At dinner, when Roger rode in after a long day, he and Dad would often talk about Sam.

"Have you heard from Sam this week?"

"No. But when he called a couple of weeks ago he sounded pretty excited about a new investment development that looked encouraging."

"Do you know these contacts of his? Can they be trusted?"

"I don't know them at all. But Sam seems to feel they will help him."

Weeks went by. Contact with Sam came more and more seldom. Months passed. Winter came and went, and spring on the ranch was always a busy time. There were fences to mend, new calves to watch, and fields to plow.

At dinner one evening Roger sensed his father was troubled. When he inquired about it, he said, "Well, it's probably nothing. But when Sam called this afternoon I got the distinct impression that he was trying awfully hard to assure me that he was okay and that his business ventures were going well. I have this gut feeling that something is wrong."

The lead story on the evening news that night reported the widespread failures of several savings and loan institutions in the metropolitan area where Sam was living. Prominent bankers and investors in those institutions had been caught in a sting operation, which linked them to underworld crime figures and drug smuggling from South America. Sam's father sat watching half-heartedly when suddenly he thought he recognized the back of Sam's head as they showed several men being lead in handcuffs from the police station.

His heart beat wildly as he sat on the edge of the couch, staring at the television screen. He tried to dismiss the picture from his mind as he finally went to bed, but over and over it played in his mind. At 6:00 A.M. the telephone rang. "Dad?"

It was Sam.

"Sam! Are you all right, Where—?"

"Dad! I have just one telephone call. I am in jail and everything has fallen in on top of me. My money is gone in an investment deal that went sour. I'm afraid I have been pretty stupid. When I realized the extent of my partner's involvement with crime, it was too late to pull out. Now I'm in over my head and don't know what to do. I'm scared, Dad. What can I do?"

Just then Roger burst into the room. "Did you see the morning news?" Sam's in jail for embezzlement and conspiracy to smuggle drugs. I'm mortified! My brother has ruined our family name forever!"

More months passed. A federal grand jury indicted Sam along with the others involved. Now, eighteen months later, the trial was beginning.

Sam's father watched the paper and television for news about the trial. Details were sketchy. Reporters seemed more delighted to share sensational tidbits about wild parties and well-known Hollywood starlets who were seen with the bankers at expensive clubs and resorts. Meanwhile, life at the ranch went on. Roger refused to discuss Sam or the trial, wanting to forget Sam altogether. He had written him off as a black sheep, and often bitterly voiced, "I hope he never shows his face around here again!"

The trial slowly ground to a conclusion. Sam was sentenced to fifteen years in jail. Fifteen years is a long time. A baby practically grows into a man in fifteen years. Every day of every one of those years Sam's dad prayed for his son in prison. Winters came and went. Dad kept on praying.

Finally the day of Sam's release arrived. He telephoned the ranch. "Dad! I've served my time and I've been released. Would it be okay if I came home to see you for a few days?"

"Okay?" his dad shouted. "Yes, it's okay! I'm waiting on you!"

"Then I'll be arriving on flight 243 at 8:11 P.M. Can you meet me or shall I get a cab?"

"Don't get a cab. I'll be there!"

Nothing could have kept Dad away from the airport. He arrived an hour early, and paced the red carpeted hallway alongside Gate four. He saw the plane still many miles out, silhouetted against the sunset sky. He watched the plane grow larger and blink on the landing lights like three diamonds strung together in the sky. He saw the plane take form in the darkness, flash by the windows, and send up little puffs of smoke as the wheels hit the runway. The whine of the engines was music to his ears. The plane seemed to take forever to taxi to the gate. Finally it pulled in, and the bell jangled on the loading platform as it moved against the door. Passengers began walking down the jetway toward him. He craned his neck, standing on one foot and then the other. Then he saw Sam. He left a boy of twenty. He was now thirty-seven.

He yelled while waving his hand high in the air, "Sam! Sam!"

Sam saw his father and started to jog. They ran toward each other, dodging passengers and luggage. Sam dropped his briefcase and his dad threw his arms around him in a tight embrace, lifting him off the floor. "Sam, thank God, Sam! I can't tell you how good it is to see you."

While they were driving home Sam began to apologize.

"Dad, I'm so sorry. I never should have messed around with those people. I ignored my better judgment and every business principle you taught me. I was greedy, and I thought I could never be caught. I know I have disappointed you and Roger, and I've dragged our family name through the mud. I won't plan to stay long, and I won't blame you if you never forgive me."

His dad drove along silently, his eyes swimming, tears spilling down his suntanned face. "All I care about is that you're home, Sam. I just thank God ..." his voice broke. They drove on in silence.

As they rounded the last bed before the ranch, Sam noticed that the driveway was full of cars. "Good grief, Dad, has Roger gone social on me or something? He must be having a party!"

They pulled into the driveway. A yellow, four-foot-by-six-foot sign sat on the lawn, with flashing lights at the top. In big six-inch letters it proclaimed, "Welcome Home, Sam!" All the lights were on. The house was packed with friends and neighbors. Big banners hand lettered with felt markers shouted from every room: "We love you, Sam." and "Welcome Home!" Sam stood in the doorway and wept. Someone started singing, "For he's a jolly good fellow."

Everyone was there except Roger. He finally showed up at 2:00

in the morning. All the guests had gone and the house was quiet. His dad was just turning out the lights when he appeared in the doorway, "Wish you could have been here, Roger," he said.

Roger was blazing mad. "Look!" he shouted. "All these years I've been slaving for you and never once have I disobeyed your orders. Yet you never gave me even a birthday party. But when this son of yours who has squandered your property with gangsters comes home, you invite the whole neighborhood!"

"Roger," his father said, a pained look on his face. "You are always with me, and everything I have is yours. But we had to celebrate and be glad, because this brother of yours was dead and is alive again; he was lost and is found."

What Biblical Truths About Creating Strong Families Does this Story Teach Us?

It's Okay to Be Imperfect

We are born into families and each family member is unique. Every family has its own pattern created by the personalities of parents and children, and also by traditions passed down from generation to generation. God apparently likes this setup since Jesus was born into a family, too. I'm impressed by the fact that Jesus never implies, while telling this story, that the family fabric is perfect or unusual. In other words, brothers get upset at brothers, people make poor choices, and life, as they say, goes on. If it's wrong to spend your life wishing you were like somebody else, it's just as wrong to spend your life wishing your family had the pattern of another family. Families, like people, are one of a kind. They are to be cherished in their own right. Families, like people, are never perfect. This story teaches us that God's love works within imperfect families.

Value the Person, Not the Action

No matter what his sons do, the father of the prodigal never acts as though their actions might jeopardize his relationship to them. This is tough love. This is the kind of love God shows us. We must learn to love like this! How tragic if our relationships with our marriage partners were so fragile that they could be fractured should we displease them! None of us would stay married for more than a few months! (Isn't this in fact what is happening across the country?) All of us, children especially, need to know we are valued as persons of profound worth, even if we misbehave or make poor choices. (By the way, most of us will do a fair share of both of these.)

A couple sought advice from their pastor. Their son (a stepson to the father) was giving them all kinds of trouble. The stepfather's method of dealing with the boy's misbehavior was to withdraw all attention and affection until the boy complied with his wishes. The boy's response was to become more and more uncontrollable. Obviously the stepfather's tactics were not working. For more than an hour the pastor compared God's love for us to what the man was suggesting. But the stepfather was adamant. To give love "indiscriminately," as he put it, rewarded and reinforced unruly behavior.

The stepfather's dilemma was this: he was confusing love of the person with approval of their actions. What he simply could never comprehend is that love is not a reward. It is a gift.

The Father Had Redemption on His Mind

The prodigal's father represents God, our Father. Since the scriptures teach that Jesus was the preexistent creator of the world,[30] and since he's the one telling us this story, we must assume that God planned from the beginning to redeem us. The implication? God values us so highly that, even though he knew we'd mess up, it didn't deter him. It still doesn't deter him. God has redemption on his mind. "You see, at just the right time, when we were still powerless, Christ died for the ungodly. Very rarely will anyone die for a righteous man, though for a good man someone might possibly dare to die. But God demonstrates his own love for us in this: While we were still sinners, Christ died for us."[31] Aren't you glad we have a father like this? Don't your children deserve parents like this?

How many parents have redemption on their minds? Wouldn't this change everything? If children knew they could not lose their parent's love, they would share their fears and failures. As parents we must offer our approval fully and freely, and not make it dependent on school grades earned or games won. Our goal should be to fill our kids' cups of self-esteem so full every day that the world cannot drain it away. Over and over we must affirm to them how valuable they are. To do this we must adjust our schedules and priorities. You can't convince someone they are of value to you unless you spend time with them, enter their world. Obviously we cannot attend school with them and they wouldn't want us tagging along when they're teenagers. But we can and must talk to them.

My wife, Karon, is a master at communication with our children. She was always available. As they moved from childhood to adolescence, the bridges of communication she built during their junior years accessed a steady stream of communication. Whenever the kids got in at night, she would be waiting. She shared in the disappointments of their day and the joys of personal victories. At times they would wake her up in the wee hours of the morning. They knew they were always welcome. Now, as adults, the lines of communication remain strong. They are not dependent on her, nor she them. But they love each other.

A PARTNERSHIP THAT WORKS

Strong families express God's love through the human touch. It's a partnership. No amount of "spiritual feeling" can replace the human touch. We can only understand God's love when another human being expresses it. Because this is so, God wrapped himself in a human body and walked with us. We couldn't have grasped it any other way. Our parents and our children depend on us to interpret God's love to them.

This will only happen if we, ourselves, walk closely with God. Each of us must guard our hearts against the swelling currents of materialism and immorality. We must consistently examine our motives and habits. We must moor ourselves to the scriptures with personal, regular study. Daily we must invite Jesus to walk with us where we walk, to lie where we lie, and to work where we work. No one on his death bed ever said, "I wish I had spent more time at the office." Many people, though, wished they had spent more time with their families. And many more wished the had spent more time with God.

113

QUESTIONS FOR DISCUSSION

1. In light of contemporary studies in psychology and science, can we still consider the Bible as the ultimate resource for sound teaching on marriage and family matters? Why?

2. Do you agree with the statement, "Love alone is not a satisfactory reason to say, 'I do.' "? What about Paul's comments in Ephesians 5:33?

3. Do you agree that Christian young people should not date non-Christians? What about Christians marrying non-Christians? Where do you draw the line, and for what reasons?

4. Discuss this statement as it relates to communication between husband and wife: "I have found that it is not when we are most lofty-minded but when we are most human that we come closest to God."

5. If both husband and wife are Christians, won't they automatically get along? Why or why not?

6. Do you agree with the author's premise that 1 Corinthians 13 and the parable of the prodigal son are sound scriptural bases for raising a Christian family?

7. Many Christians are afraid that showing love implies we approve of a person's actions or lifestyle. Was the father of the prodigal son approving his lifestyle by welcoming him? How should Christian parents handle children who choose to act and live in un-Christian ways?

NOTES

1. That is, the customs of the day during the times when the Bible was written.

2. As outdated and offensive as this may seem to us, we must realize that Hebrew culture was light years ahead of similar cultures of the day.

3. Mark 3:31–34

4. Deuteronomy 6:4–9

5. Hebrews 12:7–11

6. Hebrews 13:4

7. Leviticus 20:10

8. Hosea 1:2

9. Isaiah 62:5

10. Ephesians 5:25–27

11. Revelation 19:7

12. Barbara Dafoe Whitehead, "Divorce and Kids: The Evidence Is In," *Reader's Digest*, (July 1993), 118.

13. Dafoe 118

14. p. 119

15. p. 120–121

16. John Bradshaw. *Homecoming–Reclaiming and Championing Your Inner Child* (New York: Bantam Books), 1990.

17. Luke 14:28–30

18. Amos 3:3

19. *Candide* (Permission requested)

20. 2 Corinthians 6:14–15

21. Ephesians 5:21

22. 1 Corinthians 13:4–8

23. v. 6

24. v. 5

25. v. 6

26. Matthew 12:25–26

27. Paul Tournier, "When I Dared to Share Myself," *The Guideposts Treasury of Hope*, (Carmel, NY: Guideposts Associates, Inc: 1976), 125–127.
28. Frank Charles Thompson, ed., *The New Chain Reference Bible*, fourth edition, (Indianapolis: B. B. Kirkbridge Bible Company, Inc, 1964. "Condensed Cyclopedia of Topics and Texts," #1629, 63.
29. Based on Luke 15:11–32
30. Colossians 1:15–17
31. Romans 5:8–9

6

God Is Speaking: Pursue Holiness

Hebrews 12:14–17

"Make every effort to ... be holy; without holiness no one will see the Lord" (Hebrews 12:14).

Erosion

In his book, *The Quest for Character*,[1] Charles Swindoll tells of a favorite vacation spot off the Gulf of Mexico. His grandfather's cottage fronted a little bay where, throughout Chuck's adolescent years, his family spent summer vacations boating, swimming, jumping off piers, shrimping, fishing, floundering, and especially laughing and relaxing.

One summer, after his junior high class had studied erosion, Chuck decided to try an experiment. His junior high teacher had done a good job of convincing him that, even though we cannot see much happening or hear many warnings, erosion can occur right under our eyes. Just because it's silent and slow doesn't mean it isn't devastating. So, the last day of their summer vacation, he drove a big stake deep into the soil and then stepped off the distance between the stake and the sea. It was about fifteen feet.

The next summer Chuck returned to the stake and stepped off the distance: a little under twelve feet remained. He writes, "The bay had gobbled up another three-plus feet—not in big gulps, understand, but an inch here and another inch or so there during the year that had passed. A downward spiral was underway. I've often wondered if I ever returned to that place of happy family memories, would the cottage still be standing, or would it have surrendered to the insatiable appetite of the sea?"[2]

The culture of the 1990s in the United States is very different from what it was in the 1950s. How is it that where God was once revered he is now scorned? That where purity was praised it is now ridiculed? How is it that journalists today typically characterize Christians as "poor, uneducated, and easy to command"?[3] How is it that forty years ago the biggest problems in our public schools were talking, chewing gum, making noise, and running in the halls, but today the biggest discipline problems are rape, robbery, assault, vandalism, and drug abuse?[4] How is it that any suggested code of ethics or decency is labeled censorship and repression?

We are now seeing the effects of a fifty-year erosion of our national heart and mind. Just as the gentle gulf waters quietly stole three feet from the shoreline of Chuck Swindoll's vacation house in one year, the character of our nation has been silently eroding for decades. Bit by bit the invisible moral and ethical germs have invaded our minds and hearts. "It's slower than a clock and far more silent. There are no chimes, not even a persistent ticking. One oversight here, a compromise there, a deliberate looking the other way, a softening, a yawn, a nod, a nap, a habit ... a destiny."[5]

The Pattern of Decline

Almost fifty years ago, sociologist Carle Zimmerman compared the disintegration of various cultures with the parallel decline of family life in those cultures. He identified eight specific patterns of household behavior that epitomize the downward spiral of each culture:

- Marriage loses its sacredness, is frequently broken by divorce.
- Traditional meaning of the marriage ceremony is lost.
- Feminist movements abound.
- An increased public disrespect for parents, adults, and authority in general.

•Acceleration of juvenile delinquency, promiscuity, and rebellion.

•Refusal of people with traditional marriages to accept family responsibilities.

•Growing desire for and acceptance of adultery.

•Increasing interest in and spread of sexual perversions and sex-related crimes.[6]

The last one generally marks the final stage of societal disintegration.

We are observing the inevitable and chilling effects of sin. Tragically, this story is as old as humankind. Paul's description of society in his day sounds startlingly contemporary:

> For although they knew God, they neither glorified him as God nor gave thanks to him, but their thinking became futile and their foolish hearts were darkened. Although they claimed to be wise, they became fools, and exchanged the glory of the immortal God for images....
>
> They exchanged the truth of God for a lie, and worshiped and served created things rather than the Creator....
>
> Furthermore, since they did not think it worthwhile to retain the knowledge of God, he gave them over to a depraved mind, to do what ought not to be done. They have become filled with every kind of wickedness, evil, greed and depravity. They are full of envy, murder, strife, deceit and malice. They are gossips, slanderers, God-haters, insolent, arrogant and boastful; they invent ways of doing evil; they disobey their parents; they are senseless, faithless, heartless, ruthless. Although they know God's righteous decree that those who do such things deserve death, they not only continue to do these very things but also approve of those who practice them.[7]

Recently I read about an aggressive fungus that exists in the rain forests of South America. Ingested by ants with their food, it multiplies like wildfire within the animals' body, feeding voraciously on their vital fluids. Within days it completely overpowers its hapless victims, stopping them like statues in their tracks and sprouting hideously like small trees from their corpses. So sin gallops through cultures and nations, ruining and eroding from within.

GOD CALLS US TO LEAVE THE DARKNESS

Which level of the downward spiral has our society reached? The story of Sodom and Gomorrah from Genesis 19 is a graphic picture of God's abhorrence toward sin and his ultimate judgment against it. The calling out of Abraham's nephew, Lot, and his family, foreshadows the miraculous redemption provided by Christ from a world ravaged by sin and careening toward destruction.

Has our culture today yet sunk to the level of those ancient cities, Sodom and Gomorrah, whose very names are synonymous with degeneracy and evil? We learn from the biblical account that their immorality stank like an open sewer. Here was a hotbed of obscenity and pornography where aggressive homosexual acts were openly practiced and performed. Bestiality was common. Newcomers to the city were unsafe when they spent the night, even as a guest in someone's home! Everyday conversations reeked with lewdness and lust. No sexual activity was off limits or too base to be practiced.

God's assessment was that the inhabitants of Sodom and Gomorrah were so sickeningly infected with depravity that they were irredeemable. He planned to irrevocably destroy the cities to cleanse the world of their stench.

Before carrying out his program, God sent messengers to rescue Lot and his family, who had lived among the Sodomites for years. God's messengers declared, "The outcry to the Lord against its people is so great that he has sent us to destroy it."[8] It was hard for Lot and his family to imagine things were all that bad. They had grown used to degeneracy. When Lot urged his sons-in-law to flee with them, they thought he was joking.[9] Lot kept stalling. Finally the angels grasped him and his wife and daughters by the hands and literally dragged them out of the city. Once outside the city limits, their instructions were blunt, "Flee for your lives! Don't look back, and don't stop anywhere in the plain! Flee to the mountains or you will be swept away!"[10]

As destruction rained down behind them, Lot's wife decided to look just one more time. Perhaps she was thinking, "Nuts to your fanatical beliefs. I'm going to have just one more look!" That was the last look she ever took.

The Call to Christians

Scripture teaches that sin separates us from God. We know this—don't we? "The Bible takes sin in dead seriousness. Unlike many modern religionists, who seek to find excuses for sin and to explain away its seriousness, most of the writers of the Bible had a keen awareness of its heinousness, culpability, and tragedy. They looked upon it as no less than a condition of dreadful estrangement from God.... Apart from God, man is a lost sinner, unable to save himself or find true happiness."[11] The great prophets of the Old Testament foresaw the glorious moment when sin's horrible toll would be paid by another, and we could finally be united with God. Isaiah writes, "The people walking in darkness have seen a great light.... For to us a child is born, to us a son is given."[12] He continues "he was pierced for our transgression, he was crushed for our iniquities; the punishment that brought us peace was upon him, and by his wounds we are healed. We all, like sheep, have gone astray, each of us has turned to his own way; and the Lord has laid on him the iniquity of us all."[13]

Jesus is quoted in John 3:3: "Unless a man is born again, he cannot see the kingdom of God." In verse 16 we read, "For God so loved the world that he gave his one and only Son, that whoever believes in him shall not perish but have eternal life.... Whoever believes in him is not condemned, but whoever does not believe stands condemned already because he has not believed in the name of God's one and only Son."[14]

God is dead serious about sin. He came into sin-city and grasped us by the hand to pull us to safety. We know this—don't we? Those of us who have accepted Christ's sacrifice and turned our backs on sin are committed to living a different kind of life, a life in which Christ is glorified. We take seriously Paul's caution, "Let us purify ourselves from everything that contaminates body and spirit, perfecting holiness out of reverence for God."[15] The writer of Hebrews counsels, "Make every effort to live in peace with all men and to be holy; without holiness no one will see the Lord."[16]

The "Lot's Wife Syndrome"

It is tragic that Lot's wife wasn't the last person to take God's commands with a grain of salt. Some of us, after being pulled to safety, cannot help gazing again at Sodom with longing in our eyes. Erosion eats away the very heart of the careless Christian, who gradually becomes desensitized to sin and its effects. Paul warned Christians in Romans 2:4, "Do you show contempt for the riches of his kindness, tolerance and patience, *not realizing that God's kindness leads you toward repentance?*" (italics added). He gets specific in verses 21–23: "You, then, who teach others, do you not teach yourself? You who preach against stealing, do you steal? You who say that people should not commit adultery, do you commit adultery? You who abhor idols, do you rob temples? You who brag about the law, do you dishonor God by breaking the Law?"

The "Lot's Wife Syndrome" is reaching epidemic proportions. Many Christians today think much the way she did: God can't be serious! Surely God doesn't really mean it when he says "Do not love the world or anything in the world."[17] Purity? Who wants it? R-rated films? Everybody's going to see them. Holiness? It's not that important.

A more subtle but equally precarious position is taken by those who, like the Pharisees, keep the letter of the law but whose hearts are far from God. They erect walls of self-righteousness between themselves and holiness. Their actions are impeccable. Jesus' response to the Pharisees was not that their lifestyle had no value. It was insufficient. Jesus was looking for an attitude the scriptures describe as a contrite heart. Today's Pharisee equivalents don't drink, smoke, or swear. But their rigid legalism freezes our congregations into a perpetual winter. In the unlikely event that such Christians consider their position, they might think, God surely can't be serious when he says to love sinners!

God Is Serious about Holiness

I try to be a positive person. Being positive helps you deal more effectively with life. It helps to overlook the bad and concentrate on the good. Using different language helps: you know, "Don't call it a problem. Call it an opportunity!" It's easier to get along with some folks if you approach them cheerfully and give them the benefit of the doubt. "He must be having a hard day," we tell ourselves, preparing to put our best foot forward with a cranky, short-tempered colleague at work.

Sin, though, is never positive. It cannot be put in a good light, or made more palatable to God if we joke about it. Dr. Henry Brandt, speaking at the Southern Convention one year, made this excellent analogy. Suppose you went to the dentist with a terrible toothache. And suppose that your dentist, upon examining your mouth, said, "You have thirty-one excellent teeth here. We'll concentrate on those, and ignore this abscess in the back." Such advice is utter nonsense and totally irresponsible. A dentist who would say such a thing has no business practicing dentistry, and you wouldn't put up with such dangerous counsel. You can't be positive about an abscess. You've got to get rid of it. Drain the infection or it will kill you!

To enter the Kingdom we must forsake sin. C. S. Lewis said, "We cannot keep the tiniest souvenir of hell, no matter how intimate or inconsequential it may seem."

Who Makes the List of What "Sin" Is?

To create a list of dos and don'ts has always been a problem and is becoming more complex every year. Why so? After all, the Bible is very clear about some things, such as murder, adultery, and witchcraft. Paul even goes so far as to name specific sins in Romans 1:21–31.

Here are some of the difficulties:
1. Some things are not named specifically as sins in scripture but obviously should qualify. Who's to say?
2. Does disposition count? Typically, we Christians are quick to

point out the actions that qualify as sin, but we are slow to recognize the attitudes that Paul also names. A quick rundown of what Romans 1 classifies as sin includes greed, envy, strife, deceit, malice, arrogance, insolence, pride, ruthlessness, and heartlessness. The measurement of such things is uncertain and inexact.

3. Cultures change:

•Some admonitions of Paul no longer seem relevant because of cultural change over the last two thousand years: for instance, his lengthy plea for women to keep their heads covered in church.[18]

•America of the 1990s is very accepting of attitudes and activities that were labeled as sin twenty or thirty years ago. Some Christians creating a list of sins today might go so far as to omit traditionally off-limit activities, such as premarital sex.

A greater concern with creating a list of sins, supposedly to then avoid, is that to do so encourages legalism and undermines our personal relationship with God, which is both the launching pad for holy living and mission control for the duration of life.

How Do We Then Define Sin?

Rich Willowby told me the other day that as a child he went to the altar every Sunday, and sometimes twice each Sunday! His tender heart was constantly stirred by the exhortations to the "saints." (At one point his pastor told him he could not come forward for a whole month.) Was Rich really responding every Sunday to a Holy Spirit summons to get rid of sin? Not likely, since he had already given his heart to the Lord. Once we're a Christian, is sin a problem?

John tells us, "I write this to you so that you will not sin. But if anybody does sin, we have one who speaks to the Father in our defense—Jesus Christ, the Righteous One."[19] What is sin? A crystallization of biblical teaching about sin divides it into two types: (1) a willful transgression against God and (2) missing the mark.[20] Once we accept Christ, our attitude should be one of eager submission to God's will. With such an attitude, "willful transgression against God," although not out of the realm of possibility, is unlikely. For any number of reasons, however, we can make foolish choices, carelessly adopt a destructive habit, or unwisely enter into a relationship that will severely test our kingdom values. Such actions push us to the brink from which we can slide into sin. Here, as I see it, is where a huge number of Christians slowly succumb to the enemy's persuasion. Listen again to Swindoll's statement. "It's slower than a clock and far more silent. There are no chimes, not even a persistent ticking. One oversight here, a compromise there, a deliberate looking the other way, a softening, a yawn, a nod, a nap, a habit ... a destiny."[21]

Let me give you a true example. A young girl of twenty-two sat in her pastor's office. She was crying. The night before she had lost her virginity, and she had never even intended to do it. How did it happen? She had been studying with some friends at an all-night restaurant: her girlfriend who was also her roommate and a young man they both knew. About 3:00 P.M. they decided they'd had enough. It was time to go home. For some reason she couldn't remember, they offered to let the young man spend the rest of the night in their apartment. He could sleep on the floor. Later that morning, while her girlfriend was still sleeping, she felt the young man touch her. Not wanting to awaken her friend, she said nothing, submitting to his advances and pretending to be asleep. As incredible as it sounds, it was all over in a matter of moments.

How did this happen? Did this young woman commit a sin? Was this a willful transgression? Was it "missing the mark"? The problem, as I see it, was sheer foolishness. She unwisely invited a man to spend the night in her apartment. (No one even raises an eyebrow these days if single young people sleep together. What could happen?) Even if her girlfriend had encouraged it, she could have said no. (If my girlfriend doesn't object, I don't want to cause a scene.) She then allowed embarrassment to keep her from stopping what was surely not inevitable. (He can't be doing what I think he's doing. I don't know what to do. I'll just do nothing.) The enemy pushed her off the edge, but she walked to the brink of her own accord. Yes, I say. It was sin.

To forsake sin in this case is more than just not losing virginity. To forsake sin means that you keep yourself out of sin's way. We must use our minds as well as our hearts. We must seek the supernatural wisdom and strength of the Holy Spirit, for "our struggle is not against flesh and blood, but against the rulers, against the

125

authorities, against the powers of this dark world and against the spiritual forces of evil in the heavenly realms. Therefore put on the full armor of God, so that when the day of evil comes, you may be able to stand your ground and after you have done everything, to stand."[22]

A Biblical Strategy to Forsake Sin

> Do not love the world or anything in the world. If anyone loves the world, the love of the Father is not in him. For everything in the world—the cravings of sinful man, the lust of his eyes and the boasting of what he has and does—comes not from the Father but from the world. The world and its desires pass away, but the man who does the will of God lives forever.[23]

We must have our wits about us to figure out what "the world" means. Clearly we are told to leave it alone. But what is it?

1. "The world" encompasses the obvious sins. A couple of paragraphs ago I warned against the futility of creating a list of specific sins, the avoidance of which will achieve holiness. At the risk of sounding somewhat contradictory, every Christian must be familiar with those things the Bible categorically declares as sinful. For example, infidelity to a spouse can never be anything but sinful. It cannot be rationalized or explained away. No matter what society claims, it is wrong. Countless Christians only intended to flirt with the idea of an affair. The possibility was barely cracked open in their mind, but that was the hole in the dam that brought it crashing down around their marriage and destroyed their home.

The only way to know what the Bible teaches is to read it for ourselves.

2. "The world" encourages idolatry. The enemy is fiendishly clever and we tend to underestimate both his cunning and our weaknesses. We are like sheep, who nibble themselves lost. The tuft of grass in front of our noses seems so seductive. Gradually, following our stomachs instead of listening to the Spirit, we distance ourselves from the Master until we can no longer hear his voice. We no longer even want to hear God's voice. Another convenience for the home, one more vote, just one more investment. "God wouldn't want me to do without this," we rationalize. "Surely he wouldn't expect me to give to the needy in my community if it would inconvenience me." And so we gradually substitute the creation for the Creator.

3. "The world" dulls our spiritual fervor. This occurs on many levels. At its most innocent, our minds are cluttered with innocuous material. We fill our heads with recipes and sports. We start and end the day with a steady diet of television news. Conversations deal with business, weather, and the stock market. Such things in themselves are not wrong, but they are filling, leaving no room for anything else, particularly for a meaningful devotional life.

We move from clutter to contamination when we open our minds to people and entertainment with questionable values. We are quickly seduced and acculturated to selfishness and sin. Profanity no longer offends us. Violence seems commonplace. Sexual innuendoes fill our music and overflow television and radio. We find ourselves considering and even experimenting with habits we formerly would have avoided. Social drinking may enter the picture. Or pornographic material. Isn't it normal? we think.

Below this hazardous stage lies disaster: so long exposed, we lose our perspective altogether. Having lived in Sodom for so long, we can't quite believe that the things we have learned to enjoy are all that bad for us. Flinging good judgment aside, we start the extramarital affair. We stop attending church. We defect to the enemy. We give in to the temptation, cheat on our income taxes or engage in questionable business deals.

Peter impresses upon us the Bible's first-line strategy: leave the world alone. Abandon the things that divert your attention from a pure and holy lifestyle: "Therefore, dear friends, since you already know this, be on your guard so that you may not be carried away by the error of lawless men and fall from your secure position."[24] In the next verse a second and more wonderful strategy then comes into play: walk in the light: "But grow in the grace and knowledge of our Lord and Savior Jesus Christ. To him be glory both now and forever."[25]

GOD CALLS US TO WALK IN THE LIGHT

It is not enough to leave the bad, we must embrace the good. Paul counsels in Ephesians 5:8, "For you were once darkness, but now you are light in the Lord. Live as children of light." He continues with the two-pronged approach: have nothing to do with deeds of darkness, instead, be filled with the Spirit.[26]

Jesus himself underscored this truth when he told about the man cleansed from an evil spirit but not filled with the Holy Spirit. The evil spirit returned to his former host, bringing companion spirits more wicked than itself to take up residency.[27] The Holy Spirit gives us birth into the Kingdom and then serves as our personal guide for the duration of life. The most enriching, enjoyable, and energizing experiences on our road to holiness spring from our personal relationship with God. If disloyalty to God is the great thief of Christian achievement, then loyalty to God will help you become a distinctive, fruitful Christian.

Misconceptions about Holiness

People love to measure and compare everything. We measure our kids to see how tall they are. We measure our standard of living to determine whether or not we're successful. We measure our waistlines to judge our beauty. While such judging is disappointing, it is not surprising that many Christians try to measure holiness. We run into the same difficulties here that we do when we try to establish an official list of sins, but that doesn't keep us from trying. This measurement mania has produced some common misconceptions about holiness.

Holiness Misconception 1: the Super Christian
Jesus told us that our goal should be perfection.[28] Believers who are serious about separating themselves from the world in order to embrace a Christlike lifestyle strive to live above sin. Anything less, of course, is not worthy of our Lord. We know that we must be

filled with the Holy Spirit in order to accomplish this. Furthermore, we have God's promise that we will be transformed into the likeness of Christ "when he appears."[29]

However, when the equation is written, "Sanctification = no more sin, period," we have changed a goal Christ gives us into a command for immediate achievement. The scenario goes like this: (1) We accept Christ as Savior. (2) We realize that we are unable to live the Christian life without the help of the Holy Spirit. (3) We seek sanctification, "claiming" perfection in the same manner we might "claim" divine healing. (4) We later actually experience some unholy attitudes, make a poor choice, or collapse in the face of temptation. (5) We have no recourse since a sanctified Christian does not sin. Therefore (6) we cover them up, repress them, or give them righteous-sounding names ("I'm not angry, I'm righteously indignant"). Or (7) we assume we did not receive the Holy Spirit after all, and we try all over again. The Christians produced by this line of thought are either hypocrites who never admit imperfection or self-declared failures who feel personally responsible that they are imperfect.

The Holy Spirit most certainly has the power to help us live above sin. The Spirit isn't the problem. The problem is a self-imposed expectation, or one imposed on us by others, that to be holy means we will never sin again. "I write this to you so that you will not sin. But if anybody does sin, we have one who speaks to the Father in our defense—Jesus Christ, the Righteous One."[30]

Holiness Misconception 2: the Super Gift

It may be divine healing. Or speaking in tongues. Whatever specific gift is elevated, its presence and (successful) practice often becomes the yardstick by which the holy life is "proved" successful. At times an entire Christian body will emphasize one gift and claim that the practice of that gift is evidence of the Holy Spirit, and therefore, evidence of holiness. At other times those who use certain gifts are held somewhat in awe. This more or less creates a hierarchy of the holy and the not so holy within the church body.

It is easy to see how Christians would desire the more visible gifts, and how those gifts could elevate them in the eyes of their peers. It is not easy to find scriptural foundation for such a view, however. Scripture clearly lays forth the purpose for spiritual gifts. Paul discusses them at length in 1 Corinthians 12–14, concluding that their purpose is to build up the entire Christian community.[31] Jesus teaches that the purpose of the Holy Spirit's coming is to remind us of what (Jesus) taught, to testify about him (Jesus), and to glorify God.[32]

Nowhere do we find evidence that every Christian will receive the same gift(s). In fact, just the opposite is true: "all these [spiritual gifts] are the work of one and the same Spirit, and he gives them to each man, just as he determines."[33] Paul's further discussion, and especially his rhetorical questions in 1 Corinthians 12:29–31, imply that God bestows spiritual gifts at his own discretion with no guarantee for any person how the final tally will come out.

The biblical evidence of holiness is spiritual fruit, not spiritual gifts. Paul discusses this in Galatians 5. How can someone with a grand and glorious "spiritual gift" have fits of rage or envy, or promote discord? Gifts are easily counterfeited. Attitudes show who's really in charge of your life.

Dr. Juan Carlos Ortiz shares an insightful illustration about spiritual gifts versus spiritual fruit. In Argentina, his land of birth, it was the custom to place Christmas gifts on the Christmas tree, among the branches. On Christmas morning he would find a package or two with his name on them. He had no influence over the contents of the package, whether it was a watch or a pair of cuff links. The gift was selected by the giver. Whether or not he and his brothers wanted the same gift had no effect on the choice of gifts. The tree had little to do with the gifts, either. The tree's job was only to display the gifts. (Everyone knows that a tree can't grow a watch!)

Trees do, however, grow fruit. It is the nature of trees to bear fruit. A gift giver cannot make a tree produce an apple or pear. Apple trees produce apples. Pear trees produce pears. Brand new trees rarely produce much fruit. Mature trees will bear a bumper crop year after year. So the mature (holy) Christian produces love, joy, peace, patience, kindness, goodness, faithfulness, gentleness, and self-control. Unlike spiritual gifts, each Christian, in time, will produce all the various fruits of the Spirit. We show by our attitudes, not our gifts, who is Lord of our lives.

130

Holiness Misconception 3: the Super Separation:
Women will wear no makeup. Men will not shave. Ordinary clothes are unsatisfactory. The use of electricity is forbidden. Jewelry is out. Hair cannot be cut. Hundreds of such regulations have been practiced by well-meaning Christians since the early days of the church. Their goal is to renounce the world and affirm their connection to Christ. Some have practiced monasticism in their attempts to keep the world at bay. Others have condemned matrimony. Some even forbade having children!

Does it make sense that although we must live in the world, we should not be like the world? Of course! Scriptures abound that counsel us to be careful of the world's allure, to walk circumspectly, to separate ourselves and live lives apart. How can we ever figure out how far we should go?

How did Jesus do it? Jesus, unlike paintings of him by twentieth century artists, did not stand out in the crowd. It's not likely he always wore a white robe while everyone else wore a brown one. He had no halo glowing over his head. In order for the Romans to recognize him, Judas had to reveal his identity with a kiss. Jesus' goal was to identify with, not to stand out from. He was welcomed at parties and seemed comfortable with sinners. He never compromised his principles, yet he somehow managed to maintain a non-threatening demeanor.

Our goal is to be like Jesus. Christ's effectiveness would have been destroyed had he worn a special Son of God outfit that no one else had on. Why then should we think it is godly to stand out like nuns at a Shriners' convention, conspicuous by the outlandish way we dress, wear our hair, or conduct our lives? Sinners must be comfortable enough with the way we look to let their guard down. It is not until we have earned their trust that we can tell them about the transforming power of Christ.

Holiness is not proven by strange clothing or eccentric lifestyle. We do not have to renounce our citizenship on the planet in order to live a holy life within our culture. We must demonstrate the redemptive and winsome attitudes of the Master. Someone wryly observed, "Sitting in a church doesn't make you a Christian any more than sitting in an oven makes you a biscuit." The same is true for clothes and hairstyles. Outward garb cannot prove holiness. Jesus had strong words for the Pharisees who emphasized an outward dress code more than a contrite heart.[34] Of course, we must always practice modesty and appropriateness.

Holiness Defies Definition. It Is a Relationship.

For centuries Christians have attempted to define holiness in terms of sins to avoid or spiritual gifts to pursue. Have you ever thought of holiness as love?

To love and be loved is one of life's purest joys. We cannot measure such love. It may inspire poems or songs. It may generate feelings that cannot be described. Yet those alone who are in the love relationship understand and fully appreciate the intertwining of hearts and sharing of intimate thoughts.

Jesus had a profound love relationship with his Father. Now and then we glimpse it in his words. At the early age of twelve, Jesus traveled to Jerusalem with his parents. On their return trip he was somehow separated from them. They finally found him at the temple with the teachers of the law. His mother, frantic by this time, cried, "Son, why have you treated us like this? Your father and I have been anxiously searching for you." Jesus' answer resonates from a deep cistern of understanding of both who he was and whose he was, "Why were you searching for me?" he asked. "Didn't you know I had to be in my Father's house?"[35]

Twenty years later Jesus and his disciples were traveling through Samaria and stopped at the well near the village of Sychar. The disciples went off in search of lunch, leaving Jesus by the well. Here he met the common-law wife who was soon transformed by their half-hour conversation. When the disciples returned, they were not only astonished to find him visiting with a woman—a Samaritan woman at that—they were astounded that Jesus had neither eaten nor had interest in eating what they brought. "Rabbi, eat something," they said. But he said to them, "I have food to eat that you know nothing about." Then his disciples said to each other, "Could someone have brought him food?" "My food," said Jesus, "is to do the will of him who sent me and to finish his work."[36]

In John 17 we overhear his impassioned conversation with God.

His words disclose the deepest emotions of trust and love: "All I have is yours, and all you have is mine."[37] This powerful relationship was an anchor that bound him to his Father with the most tender loyalty. Their shared love energized his own heart with God's deepest purposes until they were one and the same. This passion sparked the rebuke Peter heard after he had struck the high priest's servant to protect his Master: "Put your sword away! Shall I not drink the cup the Father has given me?" These words blaze with holy purpose. No hint of formal obligation clouds the brilliance of this intimate commitment. These are the words of a blood brother—and a son.

The Coming of the Holy Spirit

Haven't you longed that you could have walked with Jesus? I have. I would love to see the recognition in his eyes as he called my name. I would love to spend time with this incredible person who said, "Do not let your hearts be troubled. Trust in God; trust also in me."[38] Haven't you ached to trust someone who is utterly trustworthy? I have. I would love to share my innermost feelings with Jesus—as the disciples surely must have done—knowing he wouldn't despise me for my weaknesses and failures!

The incredible news is that I can. So can you. We need no time machine to talk with Christ. He sends his Spirit to be with us forever. Hear these welcome words: "I will not leave you as orphans; I will come to you."[39] Jesus explains that his going coincides with the Holy Spirit's coming. It's all arranged. We never have to be one moment without him.

It's so wonderful that we can barely conceive that it's true. God longs for us with the same passion Jesus and the Father longed to be together. Through Christ's atoning sacrifice the wall of sin is removed and we can rush into God's arms for an eternal reunion. How deeply satisfying that the coming of the Holy Spirit fills our longing for intimacy! No exhilaration can equal the pleasure of being finally, totally, and irrevocably accepted as we are.

This is the great gap in holiness teaching: the love relationship with Christ through the Holy Spirit transforms us. Our loyalty to Christ binds us with the same anchor that bound Jesus to his

Father with the most tender loyalty. The love shared with Christ through the Holy Spirit energizes our heart with God's deepest purposes until they are one and the same. This is not a list of dos and don'ts any more than a marriage is keeping a list of dos and don'ts. We no longer care if others think us holy or not. To "prove" holiness is pointless. Our attention is not on ourselves, but on Christ.

The Holy Spirit as Paraclete

Scripture discloses the nature of the Holy Spirit, but nowhere more helpfully than in John's use of the word paraclete, a transliteration of the Greek word παρακλετος. The basic meaning of paraclete is, "One called to the side of."[40] The reasons for which the paraclete is called are many. William Barclay offers this enlightening explanation:

> The word *paracletos* really means "someone who is called in"; but it is the reason why the person is called in which gives the word its distinctive associations. The Greeks used the word in a wide variety of ways. A para-cletos might be a person called in to give witness in a law court in someone's favor; he might be an advocate called in to please someone's cause when someone was under a charge which would issue in serious penalty; he might be an expert called in to give advice in some difficult situation. He might be a person called in when, for example, a company of soldiers were depressed and dispirited to put new courage into their minds and hearts. Always a paracletos is someone called in to help when the person who calls him in is in trouble or distress or doubt or bewilderment.
> Now the word "Comforter" (word used in the King James Version) was once a perfectly good translation. It actually goes back to Wycliffe; he was the first person to use it. But in his day it meant much more than it means now. The word "comforter" comes from the Latin word fortis which means brave; and a comforter was someone

134

who enabled some dispirited creature to be brave. Nowadays the word 'comfort' has to do almost solely with sorrow; and a comforter is someone who sympathizes with us when we are sad.

Beyond a doubt the Holy Spirit does that, but to limit the work of the Holy Spirit to that function is sadly to belittle Him. We have a modern phrase which we often use. We talk of being able to cope with things. That is precisely the work of the Holy Spirit. The Holy Spirit comes to us and takes away our inadequacies and enables us to cope with life. The Holy Spirit substitutes victorious for defeated living.[41]

How Does It Work?

One of the most memorable people in my life was Pat Blume. We first met Pat when we were lay people attending East Side Church of God in Anderson, Indiana. She and her husband, Bob, had two strapping, young boys about the age of our two oldest children. We attended the same Sunday school class with Bob and Pat. We called it the BYKOTA (Be Ye Kind One To Another) class. Many couples in that class were very serious about living dynamic Christian lives.

Karon and I signed up one Sunday to join a small group Bible study. We joined a group of five couples that included Bob and Pat. We met once a month in one of our homes on Sunday night after church. After a light supper we spent time reading and discussing the Bible. Our evenings concluded with prayer. The night we were in Pat's home I was particularly struck by her vibrant hospitality and her knack for decorating. In fact, when Karon complimented her that night on her mug collection, Pat sent one home with us. We still have it.

A year or two after our Bible study experience Pat was diagnosed with cancer. We were stunned. Why should it happen to a young Christian mother in the prime of her life? Cancer is never welcome, and its arrival in one's particular circle of friends is sobering. We all began to pray for Pat. But Pat didn't improve.

The cancer advanced from one part of her body to another.

Then shocking news shook our world: the cancer had gone to her brain. Already a veteran of various treatments, Pat was slowly wasting away. She wore a wig—you'd never guess if she hadn't told you—to hide her shiny head. She came to church in a wheel chair. Her smile never wavered.

About this time my wife, Karon, was visiting Pat in her home. As Karon tells it, the discussion got around to suffering in the Christian life. Pat had been doing a lot of thinking about it, and when there was a lull in the conversation, she said quietly. "We'll all suffer, Karon." There was no bitterness or rancor. Just peace.

As her body faded, Pat's spirit blossomed. She had said for a number of years that her goal in life was to be a "distinctive Christian." She certainly was achieving that goal. Whoever went to visit her came away with a blessing. People were won to the Lord by her wheelchair. Her radiant faith touched us all.

Why wasn't she healed? It's a haunting question that's hard to answer. She was so very close to God. Was there something better than healing going on that we couldn't quite see? What was it?

In her last months Pat had to undergo painful stretching exercises every day in order to keep breathing. After one particularly exhausting session, Betty Fair crawled up on Pat's bed next to her and took her hand. Pat whispered huskily, "Let's sing, Betty." Betty asked, "What shall we sing?" Pat didn't hesitate, "Great Is Thy Faithfulness."

Within days, Pat left us. As I think of her now, a glow comes to mind that exists every time I remember her. It is the light of holiness shining brightly. Her body wouldn't cooperate, but her spirit scaled the heights with God. A "distinctive Christian" she said. Then Pat took God's hand and walked the high road with the Spirit.

The Holy Spirit, the paracletos, became Pat's intimate companion. Together they accomplished all of God's purposes for Pat during her brief life.

Holiness is the ultimate goal. It has nothing to do with lists. It has everything to do with love.

A Psalm of Single-Mindedness
Lord of reality
make me real
not plastic
synthetic
pretend phony
an actor playing out his part
hypocrite.
I don't want
to keep a prayer list
but to pray
nor agonize to find Your will
but to obey
what I already know
to argue
theories of inspiration
but submit to Your Word.
I don't want
to explain the difference
between eros and philos
and agape
but to love.
I don't want
to sing as if I mean it
I want to mean it.
I don't want
to tell it like it is
but to be it
like you want it.
I don't want
to think another needs me
but I need him
else I'm not complete.
I don't want
to tell others how to do it
but to do it
to have to be always right
but to admit it when I'm wrong.

I don't want to be a census taker
but an obstetrician
nor an involved person, a professional
but a friend
I don't want to be insensitive
but to hurt where other people hurt
nor to say I know how you feel
but to say God knows
and I'll try
if you'll be patient with me
and meanwhile I'll be quiet.
I don't want to scorn the clichés of others
but to mean everything I say
including this.[42]

QUESTIONS FOR DISCUSSION

1. How do you perceive Christians today are being desensitized to sin?

2. How would you define *holiness?*

3. Discuss John 17:14–17 which delineates being "in the world," without being "of the world." What practical application does this have today?

4. Describe your experience with the Holy Spirit. When did you first become aware of your need for him? How do you relate this with "holiness"?

5. Do you agree with the author that holiness is a relationship more than it is the keeping of lists? Why or why not?

6. How can Christians strike a balance between living a holy life and relating to non-Christians?

7. The author discusses sin as (a) willful transgression and (b) missing the mark. What about the concept of sin as omission? (Ref. James 4:17.)

NOTES

1. Charles R. Swindoll, *The Quest for Character* (Portland, Ore: Multnomah Press, 1987), 87–88.

2. Swindoll 88

3. "Energized by Pulpit or Passion, The Public Is Calling: 'Gospel Grapevine' Displays Strength in Controversy over Military Gay Ban," Michael Weisskopf, *The Washington Post*, (1 February, 1993), A-1. Reported by *Focus on the Family*, January 1994.

4. Richard M. Swenson, *Margin* (Colorado Springs, Col: NavPress, 1992), 24.

5. Swindoll 89

6. Carle C. Zimmerman, *Family and Civilation* (New York: Harper & Brothers, 1947), 776–777.

7. Romans 1:21–23, 25, 28–32

8. Genesis 19:13

9. v. 14

10. v. 17

11. "Sin, Sinners," *The Interpreter's Dictionary of the Bible, vol. 4* (Nashville: Abingdon, 1962), 361.

12. Isaiah 9:2, 6

13. Isaiah 53: 5–6

14. John 3: 16, 18

15. 2 Corinthians 7:1

16. Hebrews 12:14

17. 1 John 2:15

18. 1 Corinthians 11:5–16

19. 1 John 2:1
20. This is, admittedly, an oversimplification of a complex subject covering the biblical writings over many centuries in both the Hebrew and Greek languages.
21. Swindoll 89
22. Ephesians 6:12–13
23. 1 John 2:15–17
24. 2 Peter 3:17
25. 2 Peter 3:18
26. Ephesians 5:11, 18
27. Luke 11:24–26
28. Matthew 5:48; however, the true meaning of the text is a promise (you shall be perfect) rather than a command for immediate perfection now and forevermore.
29. 1 John 3:2
30. 1 John 2:1–2, italics added
31. 1 Corinthians 12:7, 14–31; 14:40
32. John 14:26; 15:26; 16:14
33. 1 Corinthians 12:11
34. Matthew 23:1–36
35. Luke 2:49
36. John 4:27–34
37. John 17:10
38. John 14:1
39. vv. 16, 18
40. *International Dictionary of the Bible*, vol. 3, 654.
41. William Barclay, *Daily Bible Study Series: The Gospel of John.* (Philadelphia, Pa: Westminster Press, 1956), 194–195.
42. Joseph Bayly, "Psalm of Single-Mindedness," *Psalms of My Life.* (Wheaton, Ill: Tyndale House, 1969), 40–41.

7

God Is Speaking: Do My Will

Hebrews 13:20–21

Can we know the will of God? Yes. But it may not be what we think. I have heard many Christians confidently quote Jeremiah 29:11, "For I know the plans I have for you ... plans to prosper you and not to harm you, plans to give you hope and a future." At times I have quoted those words myself. Are God's plans, though, prewritten history? If this should be so, do they include some sort of master schedule for us and our lives? Has God chosen your marriage partner and my career ahead of time so all we have to do is plug into his will to find happiness?

Just how detailed do God's plans get, and how much does he leave up to us? Is the street on which I live a part of God's plan? Or could I live as happily in any number of neighborhoods? What about the church you attend? The songs you sing? The car your mother drives? What about clothes, or menus we prepare for our guests? The Bible does tell us that God has numbered the hairs on each of our heads.[1] But does it say that in order to please him we must pray to find the best hairstyle?

A larger question looms. Why is it that when we discuss God's will, we all think about ourselves and our lives? I suppose one could say that we're basically selfish, concerned only about our future and our families. (Our prayer requests tend to support this view.) I'm inclined to think, however, that we Christians who ponder the will of God sincerely desire to cooperate with the divine agenda. Our motivations are mostly right. But is our lens wide enough to perceive the scope of God's program?

God's Will

The Bible teaches that God created the world. It was his plan, his will. Part of that plan was to inhabit the earth with men and women. As we follow the scriptural narrative, we discover that God has definite ideas about how people should relate to one another. The social order is designed in harmony with God's character; therefore men and women must learn to deal with God on a moral basis.

God bonds himself by covenant to a chosen people and prospers them as long as they keep faith. In time God's prophets reveal that God's will includes all nations, and that all forms of nationalism and racism are inappropriate.[2] Building on the broad foundation of the prophets, the New Testament reveals that the will of God extends his kingdom to every frontier of human habitation. God's means of conquest is moral and spiritual, not physical. His pattern is never to coerce people's will, but to redeem whomever responds to his overture in Christ.[3]

Satan opposes God's plan to redeem the race, but our omnipotent Creator makes atonement for humankind in the cross of Christ, and Satan is defeated. One of the most remarkable concepts of the Bible is that God himself must suffer in order to implement God's will. God's passion for humanity shackles his omnipotent will as he beholds his own Son suffer and die on the cross.[4]

Where Do We Fit In?

This cosmic, wide-angled view of God staggers us with its breadth and power. What possible part can one person play in this vast drama that transcends nations and millennia? The truth is almost beyond belief. God employs ordinary women and men to accomplish his glorious will. God forgives our rebellion, takes us into partnership, and sends his own Spirit as a personal, twenty-four-hour guide. Hear Paul's words: "I thank Christ Jesus our Lord, who has given me strength, that he considered me faithful, appointing me to his service. *Even though I was once a blasphemer and a persecutor and a violent man,* I was shown mercy because I acted in ignorance and unbelief. The grace of our Lord was poured out on me abundantly, along with the faith and love that are in Christ Jesus."[5]

God's deepest passion is to save the world. It is God's will that you and I, who are a part of this world, believe in Jesus Christ so that we can be saved. It then is God's will that we follow his teaching: "All authority in heaven and on earth has been given to me. Therefore go and make disciples of all nations, baptizing them in the name of the Father and of the Son and of the Holy Spirit, and teaching them to obey everything I have commanded you. And surely I will be with you always, to the very end of the age."[6] According to this commandment, God's will is not something we must struggle to discern. God makes it abundantly clear. We are to adopt his goals for ourselves. We must apply our personal creativity, energy, and resources toward evangelizing others. "You are not your own; you were bought at a price."[7]

An Impossible Demand?

Is this an impossible demand God makes of us, to spend our lives and resources on his purposes?

One Sunday evening, some young people were complaining that the church was making too many demands on them, on their time, and on their finances. One of these young men grabbed the arm of an elderly gentleman who had attended the congregation for years. He heatedly fired a question, "Don't you agree that the church is making impossible demands on us and our resources?"

The old man smiled, thought for a few moments, and then replied,

"Years ago I fell in love with a beautiful young woman. After dating her for quite a while, I proposed, and she accepted. We were soon married, and began a wonderful life. We led a carefree, happy existence. We went where we wanted, and when. We hadn't a care in the world.

143

"One day we got the happy news that we were to become parents. We looked forward to that day with grand anticipation. The baby was soon born. We were so proud of our new son. We brought him home joyfully, but soon discovered that life would never be the same. With this cuddly bundle came many responsibilities we hadn't counted on: early morning feedings, diaper bags, high chairs, and unexpected messes from spilled milk and soiled clothing. That baby grew into a splendid little boy. Now we spent even more time with him, driving him to Little League baseball games and helping him with his homework. Before we knew it, he had practically grown up, and we sent him off to college. It took every dime we could scrape together, but it was worth it!

"Shortly after he began his freshman year, the dean of the university telephoned us. Our son was gravely ill, he said, and we should come immediately. We drove there as fast as humanly possible. But by the time we arrived, it was too late. He was gone forever. Sadly, we made arrangements for the burial back home, the cemetery plot, and the gravestone. Ever since then, he hasn't cost us one penny!"[8]

God's demands are not too harsh. Our love is too small. God lavishes an ocean upon us. Are we responding with only a thimbleful of gratitude and obedience?

TO DO GOD'S WILL REQUIRES OBEDIENCE

Is God concerned whether or not we do his will? Is our obedience important to him? You decide after reading the following parable. Jesus said,

> What do you think? There was a man who had two sons. He went to the first and said, "Son go and work today in the vineyard."
> "I will not," he answered, but later he changed his mind and went.
> Then the father went to the other son and said the same thing. He answered, "I will, sir," but he did not go.
> Which of the two did what his father wanted?
> "The first," they answered.

Jesus said to them, "I tell you the truth, the tax collectors and the prostitutes are entering the kingdom of God ahead of you. For John came to you to show you the way of righteousness, and you did not believe him, but the tax collectors and the prostitutes did. And even after you saw this, you did not repent and believe him."[9]

Too many of us Christians act as though we have the option of doing God's will or not. Has the ease of our lifestyles contributed to our lackadaisical attitudes about obeying God's will? Probably. With the downward spiral of morality in the United States, more and more of us will be forced to make tough choices. To do God's will requires obedience. It always has.

Obedience in Private

A man was hiking in the mountains. Suddenly he slipped and fell. Down he went over a precipice. Fortunately, a bush was growing from the other side of the rocky cliff and the man was able to grab hold of it. It was a long way up and a long way down, and all the poor man could do was hold onto that bush for dear life. In desperation he called out, "Is anyone up there?"

A booming voice answered, "Yes, this is God."

"Dear Lord, please help me!" cried the man.

"But do you trust me?" asked the voice.

"Yes, I trust you, Lord!" the man shouted.

"Then let go!" God commanded

The man paused momentarily, then shouted, "Is anyone else up there?"[10]

We laugh because we've been there, hoping against hope that there will be another way out. Abraham learned that there is no other way out, only obedience.

Abraham's Private Obedience

Have you ever put yourself in Abraham's shoes? Remember God's promise to Abraham and Sarah, that God would create a chosen people, and the seed of their two bodies would launch that race? Remember that they were already ancient, well beyond child-bearing years? It was difficult for them to believe, as the clock kept ticking, that God would bring it to pass. At one point Sarah just broke down and laughed when God's messenger reminded Abraham it would still happen.[11] She just couldn't conceive that a woman with one foot in the grave would ever have her other foot in a maternity ward!

God kept his word and the miracle child was born! How appropriate that they named him Isaac, Hebrew word for laughter! Now their days were filled with the unaccustomed joys of caring for their own newborn baby. Soon Isaac toddled around the tent. He grew into a strapping young lad with bright, inquisitive eyes and curly hair. He was the apple of his father's eye.

Then God said to Abraham, "Take your son, your only son Isaac, whom you love, and ... sacrifice him ... as a burnt offering."[12] An impossible demand? The scriptures, so brief and to the point, do not divulge the agonies that savaged Abraham's heart that night. But we can imagine the tortured conversation and questioning. Abraham had pled for Sodom. Surely he pled for Isaac's life!

In the morning the decision had been made. Abraham readied himself for the trip. As he saddled the donkey and instructed the servants who would accompany them, Isaac was watching. "Dad!" his clear young voice rang out.

"Yes, my son?"

"Where are you going?"

"On a journey, my son—a long journey."

"Dad—can I go with you?"

Abraham, struck to the heart, turned away, his eyes swimming. When he regained his composure, he gently stroked Isaac's thick hair. "Yes, Isaac. You may go."

On the third day they reached the place where they would leave the servants. Abraham and Isaac moved ahead, carrying the wood for the altar. Long shadows fell behind them in the late afternoon. Only the crunch of the stones under their sandals broke the silence. Isaac spoke up, his eager voice questioning, "Father, where is the lamb for the burnt offering?"

The old man again turned away, hiding the tears that trickled down his leathered cheeks. How could he speak it? How could he do it?

"The Lord will provide," he finally got it out. Did he know how prophetic his words would prove?

The Genesis writer paints the scene with swift strokes. "When they reached the place God had told him about, Abraham built an altar there and arranged the wood on it. He bound his son Isaac and laid him on the altar, on top of the wood. Then he reached out his hand and took the knife to slay his son."[13] With the knife poised overhead, glinting in the fading sunlight, an angel called. It was a test, only a test. With shaking arms, the father lifted his quivering son from the wood. They clung, weeping together, for a long, long time.

Thus God proves the mettle of those who would follow him. Not everyone will obey. Will we? Private obedience: only you know what God is asking. No one but you—and God—will know if you obey.

Obedience in Public

God's will also requires public obedience. Daniel, Old Testament prophet, recounts that Nebuchadnezzar, king of Babylon, besieged and captured Jerusalem. The sack of Jerusalem, Judaism's golden city, severely wounded the self-image of the Jews. The Babylonians even blasphemed the holy of holies, plundering the gold and silver from Solomon's Temple before burning it to the ground! Battle survivors were marched as slaves to Babylon. How could they ever regain their position with God? Nebuchadnezzar selected the cream of Jewish leadership to help rule his own country. Perhaps he thought he had broken their faith in God when he toppled their city. He was wrong. We recognize some names among those chosen: Daniel, Shadrach, Meshach, and Abednego.

The king built a monstrous monument in his own likeness, taller than a four-story building and made from solid gold. Daniel said it was dazzling. The king ordered all citizens to worship this statue by bowing down to it at appointed times. Anyone who dared to disobey was to be executed by fire.

A similar dilemma would later confront New Testament Christians in the Roman empire. Perhaps they drew courage from the response of Shadrach, Meshach, and Abednego. Some people of faith might rationalize that to bow down to a statue in order to save their lives is a worthy exchange. The young men from Jerusalem thought otherwise. Jerusalem was burned and only a memory, it was true. Yet the one, true God still lived and deserved their absolute loyalty. When everyone else made obeisance to the idol, they stood, unbowed.

Their disobedience was gleefully reported to Nebuchadnezzar, who called them on the carpet. He offered them a second chance to comply, which they graciously declined, saying, "If we are thrown into the blazing furnace, the God we serve is able to save us from it, and he will rescue us from your hand, O king. But even if he does not, we want you to know, O king, that we will not serve your gods or worship the image of gold you have set up."[14]

Livid with rage, Nebuchadnezzar had the three young men thrown into the furnace. Miraculously, they survived. Nebuchadnezzar gave them the ultimate acclaim with his decree, "They ... were willing to give up their lives rather than serve or worship any god except their own God."[15]

Few of us in North America have been challenged to make such a choice. Should that time come, to do God's will requires obedience.

TO DO GOD'S WILL REQUIRES ACTION

James has a gift for getting to the point: "Faith, by itself," he thunders, "if it is not accompanied by action, is dead." Lloyd Ogilvie believes that doing God's will demands audacity. Does that word surprise you? Don't let it. Check the dictionary. Its primary meaning is exhibiting an unabashed or fearless spirit.

You cannot take a correspondence course in how to ride a bicycle. You've got to take off the training wheels, get on the bike, and ride! Nor can you learn to obey God's will by sitting on the sidelines, lamely making resolutions and promises.

The Proof Is in the Pudding

A commercial jet liner was cruising at an altitude of thirty thousand feet. A businessman gazed idly at the cloud formations below. Suddenly he noticed sparks streaming from one of the engines. Horrified, he saw the engine burst into a ball of flame, and, in only a few minutes' time, separate from the wing and plummet downward into the clouds below. The plane shuddered violently and began to lose altitude. The captain's voice crackled over the intercom, advising the passengers and crew of their emergency status. The businessman clenched his eyes shut, clasped his hands, and began to pray fervently. He continued to pray until the pilot had successfully negotiated an emergency landing, at which time he opened his eyes and released his grip. Relief flooded the plane and the passengers broke into applause when the captain advised them that there was no further danger. As passengers stood to gather their belongings, the businessman again closed his eyes to pray.

As the plane emptied, a woman said, "When we were in trouble up there, I watched you pray. It helped me to get through the experience without panicking. I'm grateful that your prayer was answered. Would you mind telling me what you prayed?"

"Not at all," the man replied. "I just kept repeating, 'Lord, if you let us land safely, I'll sell all my stocks and bonds and real estate and give the money to the poor.' " Still curious, the woman asked, "What did you say the second time you prayed, after the pilot announced that we had made a safe landing and all was well?"

"Oh, I just added one word," the man replied.

"Amen?" she asked.

"No," he said. "Someday."[16]

This fellow was only fooling himself with such an insincere prayer. Such spiritual fancy footwork is entirely too commonplace. Any strongly held belief leads to action. If we are unwilling to follow through on what we say we believe, we are hypocrites of the worst kind.

"I trust the Lord," we say; but we won't tithe.

"I love you," he says; but he won't marry.

"I believe God loves everyone." she says; but she won't speak to a church visitor she has heard is a homosexual.

"I believe in forgiveness," we affirm; but we hold grudges.

Doing God's will requires more than lip service; it requires action.

Grace Isn't Cheap

It was 1939, and Hitler was gaining popular support across Germany. The Nazi party was developing an alarming momentum, which, if unchecked, would overrun Europe and perhaps the world. The celebrated German Christian, Dietrich Bonhoeffer, who had been visiting in the United States, decided not to remain in the safe refuge he had found in America that summer. He reasoned that, since he was a German Christian who did not believe that what Hitler was doing was right, faith demanded that he return to his homeland to speak out against that evil regime. He knew it might cost him his life. He was determined to go anyway.

Well-meaning Christians in the United States urged him to stay. Why should he endanger his life? Wouldn't it be a better stewardship to stay where he could write, speak, and travel on behalf of God's kingdom? Bonhoeffer said simply, "Cheap grace!"

He returned to Germany, became a part of the resistance movement, and was arrested. On April 9, 1945, one week before the Americans liberated the concentration camp where he was being held, the Nazis executed him.

His book, *The Cost of Discipleship*, is authenticated by his audacious obedience.

TO DO GOD'S WILL REQUIRES PERSEVERANCE

"Therefore, since we are surrounded by such a great cloud of witnesses, let us throw off everything that hinders and the sin that so easily entangles, and let us run with perseverance the race marked out for us."[17]

An Example of Perseverance

When he was seven years old, his family was forced out of their home on a legal technicality, and he had to work to help support thm.

At age nine, his mother died.

At 22, he lost his job as a store clerk. He wanted to go to law school, but his education wasn't good enough.

At 23, he went into debt to become a partner in a small store.

At 26, his business partner died, leaving him a huge debt that took years to repay.

At 28, after courting a girl for four years, he asked her to marry him. She said no.

At 37, on his third try, he was elected to Congress. Two years later, he failed to be re-elected.

At 41, his four-year old son died.

At 45, he ran for the Senate and lost.

At 47, he failed as the vice-presidential candidate.

At 49, he ran for the Senate again, and lost.

At 51, he was elected President of the United States. His name was Abraham Lincoln, a man many consider the greatest leader the country ever had.

Some people get all the breaks.[18]

Don't Get Sucked into the System

The world's patterns for human behavior are at sharp odds with Christian teaching, and it will take perseverance to keep from getting sucked into them. Paul advises, "Do not conform any longer to the pattern of this world, but be transformed by the renewing of your mind. Then you will be able to test and approve what God's will is–his good, pleasing and perfect will."[19]

In Romans 12:3–21 Paul outlines many dynamic features of the Christ-centered life. We find the "pattern of this world" by listing their opposites. A few of the prominent features in the world's pattern follow. (No doubt you can list many others.)

•**Depersonalization.** The church is a body every part of which we value and cherish. Over and over Paul stresses that every Christian is an invaluable member of the whole, and each is vital for the whole to survive. The world, though, judges everybody with the same cookie cutters: brains, brawn, beauty, and bank account. Way too often we Christians rank others by the world's criteria.

James whacks our knuckles with his comments: "Suppose a man comes into your meeting wearing a gold ring and fine clothes, and a poor man in shabby clothes also comes in. If you show special attention to the man wearing fine clothes and say, 'Here's a good seat for you,' but say to the poor man, 'You stand there,' or, 'Sit on the floor by my feet,' have you not discriminated among yourselves and become judges with evil thoughts?"[20] Then again, some of us tend to rank non-Christians as less valuable than Christians, as though they somehow are not real people. God values everyone.

• **Value Assigned by Appearance.** Paul counsels us in verse 9 to love with sincerity. The world loves insincerely. Harold Myra, publisher of *Christianity Today*, wrote the following unorthodox and brutally honest prayer when a young man. What a graphic portrayal of both depersonalization and shallow values!

Beasts and Beauties
Lord, I never said anything nasty,
but I admit I never accepted her—
not as an equal.
She was a spinster at seventeen,
and she always would be;
reminded me of a skinny, leafless tree
trying to grow on an expressway divider—
surrounded by concrete and grumbling cars,
roots into grass so sparse and exhaust choked,
other leaves avoided her.
Even as a little kid,
she must have been like that,
alone, avoided,
life roaring past her with no apology for the fumes.
Who hugged the girl but her mother?
Her face was angular, all bones, dark shadows,
touches of black facial hair.
I ducked to the back seat
to make sure no one got the idea
she was with me.

She became very religious
and even went off to Bible school.
I remember driving her somewhere
while she was full of joy and resolutions.
"No Bible, no breakfast," she told me,
saying how vital you were to her.
And that summer she got pregnant.
That was the end of her bright new life—
you don't go off to Bible school
with a baby in your tummy.
I wondered then, unkindly,
what hard-up misfit had touched her,
had treated her like a person,
had held her with affection,
and suddenly nothing mattered to her
as much as being
held. . . .

I don't know about that summer.
but one thing she needed
besides her Bible and prayers:
Christ come alive in friends.
Could I have touched her on the shoulder,
laughed with her?
Could the girls have been more like sisters
than Mothers Superior?
Maybe she could have found a love
that wouldn't have left her pregnant and alone.
Maybe she could have been strong,
and chosen for herself,
if she'd found more of you in some of us. . . .

How much have I grown, Lord,
beyond seeing friendship as plus or minus status coupons?
Surely I still don't act that way!
But do I find more sophisticated ways
to shun the misfit?

153

Do I love the nobody,
the social embarrassment?

Lord, help me not to be molded
by the world's ad campaign of luscious lovelies
and wind-blown men on boats and horses.
By your Spirit, help me to see
beneath skin and posture, style and hair.[21]

•Self-Centeredness

Paul's advice is to "honor one another above ourselves."[22] But the world is desperately selfish. It is easy to begin judging the world by our "To Do" lists. We judge other congregations by our congregation, other families by our family, other church groups by our church group. We fuss for attention and recognition, and play games in order to get our name in some paper or newsletter. We politick to get an honorary degree. We take comfort because we have friends in important places, or we are discouraged because we don't. We are relieved when the bad news is for someone else, and only pray for peace if our neighborhood is threatened. Self-centered? Us? Surely not!

At times we are shocked to discover where our true priorities lie. In February of 1993 Karon and I put our California house up for sale. We were going to be moving to Indiana in June, and we wanted to give God lots of opportunity to take care of this little real estate assignment. On three other occasions we sold houses in various parts of the country. God came through then, and we knew he would come through again.

It so happened that the listing of our home for sale coincided with a momentous downturn in the California economy. Whereas always before real estate in California had appreciated in value, it was suddenly depreciating. But, we comforted ourselves, God was on our side and would work a miracle. We thought.

For months we tried to (1) sell it ourselves, and (2) use the services of a "sell-it-yourself" type of company. You could have grouped all the lookers in one bathroom and still have room for a square dance.

By June we listed the home with a conventional real estate firm.

154

Now! we thought. Now the buyers will come swarming in from the hinterlands, pleading with us to sell them our beautiful house. Nope. Those buyers were somewhere else. In the meantime I moved back to Indiana and Karon stayed in California. This surely wasn't God's will, that we should be separated like this. Why didn't God do something?

I was grousing about this one day in what could loosely be called a prayer time. Frankly, I was complaining loudly about God's lack of attention to a very important matter. God interrupted my pity party with a few questions. "David," he said. "What's the worst thing that could happen to you about this house?"

Finally, I thought. I'm finally getting some attention!

"Well, if we didn't sell the house at all, we wouldn't be able to pay off the mortgage ..." I paused, waiting. Nothing. I continued, "The bank would repossess the house and our credit rating would be ruined ..."

"And...?" God interjected.

"Well ..." I didn't like the way this was going. I was beginning to sense that God's ideas and mine were very different.

God spoke again. "What would you have left?"

"Oh—well—I'd have Karon and the children. Of course, I'd still have you, and heaven, and a secure future. I'd still have my new job, which is really exciting ..."

God interrupted me. "In other words, you'd still have everything that's worthwhile?"

Wait. What was that?

"You'd have everything that is worthwhile, wouldn't you? I'll take care of this house. Leave it to me. As for you—trust me!"

I realized with a start that God's will and my will might not be exactly the same. I assumed that it was God's will to sell my house immediately—miraculously, if necessary. Why? Because I was God's child, that's why. (Note the self-centeredness here? It took me several months to find it myself.)

The house finally sold—in January of 1994. The bank did not repossess it, although we came awfully close. I'm working hard not to be so self-centered from now on. And we still have everything we need.

System-Kill in the World's Pattern

It is inherent to human nature to create "systems" of thought everywhere. Good systems of thought (what Christ taught) create Christlike behavior. Conversely, destructive thought-systems (the pattern of the world) create worldly behavior. They even may penetrate "good" places like family and church life. We must recognize that bad patterns can develop within good organizations. When worldly thought patterns infiltrate the church, Christlike behavior gradually disappears.

Most of us have no problem identifying bad patterns. We know that obsession with sex and materialism are intrinsic ingredients of the worldly system. It is much more difficult for us to recognize worldly patterns taking root in godly systems. Some congregations have been destroyed by sheer stubbornness, rigidity, and prejudice. Why? Ungodly patterns developed in godly places. Suppose good Christian people start playing politics in the church, using influence and money to secure favor and power for themselves or their friends. How can this occur? Worldly thought patterns have taken root and ultimately bear fruit.

Thought-systems so integrate into society that they take on lives of their own. They grow into commonly held social expectations and become the measuring sticks we use to judge success or failure, value or worthlessness.

Look at **Table No. 1.** Have you noticed anyone who fits the descriptions on the left side of the table? The world's patterns (on the right) are responsible.

Only constant vigilance prevents these patterns from stealing their way into our lives.

How Thought-Systems Affect Us

A naturalist recounted her experience one morning.

> I came upon a pond which lay like a green jewel among the trees. Waxed lily pads floated on the mirrored surface. Dragonflies darted from flower to flower, stitching them together with fairy wings. Lush cattails

Table #1

Example of system-kill	Mind-set that is responsible
A sense of being overwhelmed by schedule, business, and time pressures.	"Accomplishments create value. People are less important than profits."
Decay of character, integrity. Promising what we cannot produce or perhaps never intend to produce.	"What's good for me outweighs what's good for anyone else."
Prejudice toward classes, races, or types of people—homeless people or non-Christians.	"All people are not equal. People like me are the best."
Rigidity, dogmatism.	"My way is superior. I won't discuss it."
Moral feeble-mindedness; a dulled awareness of what violence and illicit sex are doing to our society.	"Tolerance above all. Every belief has equal value. Right and wrong are a personal choice."
Playing political games to achieve personal goals.	"My desires outweigh other people's rights."
Loss of passion for God. Rationalization of godlessness.	"Pleasure and human logic are adequate yardsticks to measure right and wrong."
Hypocrisy, pretending to be something you're not.	"Truth is unimportant," or "I'm not good enough so I must pretend."

flourished in the shallows. It was there I saw the little frog.

He sat motionless on a green lily pad, as though lost in thought. I drew near with caution, careful not to alarm him lest he plunge beneath the surface. Tiptoeing to within a few feet, I crouched to get a better view. It slowly dawned on me that all was not well with my amphibious companion. Never moving, his eyes stared blankly, their brightness slowly fading as though the sun were setting within his brain. His spotted skin lost its sheen. To my horror, his head began to dimple, then sag inward as though air was slowly escaping a balloon. I watched, transfixed, as his froggy shape slowly deflated.

It was then I noticed a dark shadow immediately beneath him. A huge water beetle lay submerged. I had read about these beetles, but had never witnessed one in action. Drifting underneath their prey, they latch onto them and inject a numbing chemical which renders them immobile. The potent venom then liquefies the organs and even the bones, which are sucked out.

Now his meal was finished, and without a sound the dark shape glided away. All that was left of my little friend was a green puddle of skin, floating sadly by the cattails.[23]

Saul, Victim of System-Kill

In 1 Samuel we meet Saul, an impressive man from an impressive family. Not only was his father a highly respected warrior from a family of warriors, Saul himself was known for his good looks and tall physique. God anointed him to be the first king of his fledgling nation, a big man for a huge task. At the time of his calling he was a young, charismatic leader who was sensitive to the spirit of the Lord.

In his early years he evidenced both humility and self-control. After leading his people to a resounding victory, he refused to put his enemies to death saying, "No one shall be put to death today, for this day the Lord has rescued Israel."

For forty years Saul and his armies expanded the kingdom, waging battle against the peoples around them. As the years progressed, Saul drifted from the Lord. He lost his sense of divine appointment, and gave in to the pressures of those who clamored for riches. Confusion increasingly clouded his judgment. Time and time again he performed duties reserved exclusively for God's prophet. He even broke faith with God's commandments. Tragically, he believed he was doing the right thing.

Saul had the opportunity of a lifetime, but never seemed able to grasp it. His later years were filled with jealousy and hatred. When God anointed David to succeed Saul, Saul hunted him down like an animal.

In the sunset years of his faltering monarchy, he felt more at home consulting a common medium for direction than the Lord, whom he claimed was out of reach. He ended his tragic and joyless life by falling on his own sword, an eloquent admission that he no longer believed in the God who had believed in him.[24]

TO DO GOD'S WILL REQUIRES TRANSFORMATION

The little frog was victim to natural forces it could neither control nor understand. Saul succumbed to forces he did not understand, either. Unlike the frog, Saul chose—actively or by default—to desert God. If we are to do God's will, we must not only be sharp to discern the systems of this world, we must be transformed by the renewing of our mind.[25] Only the indwelling Christ can accomplish this indispensable task.

•Refocus

Daily—sometimes hourly—we must ask ourselves, "What are my priorities?" Paul gives us an outline to develop a Christlike system of thought: "Whatever is true, whatever is noble, whatever is right, whatever is pure, whatever is lovely, whatever is admirable—if anything is excellent or praiseworthy—think about such things. What you have learned or received or heard from me, or seen in me—put it into practice."[26]

•Keep Looking at Christ

Christ must regain the central focus of our daily routine. (Read that last sentence again. Underline central focus of our daily routine.) We cannot resist this world's intense suction to assimilate and digest us without Christ's daily strength. Listen to this testimony about Moses and the reason for his achievements: "By faith, Moses, when he had grown up, refused to be known as the son of Pharaoh's daughter. He chose to be mistreated along with the people of God rather than to enjoy the pleasures of sin for a short time. He regarded disgrace for the sake of Christ as of greater value than the treasures of Egypt, because he was looking ahead to his reward. By faith he left Egypt, not fearing the king's anger; he persevered because he saw him who is invisible.' "[27]

•Persevere, and Persevere Some More

The great Christians are not those who have never failed. Just the opposite! We choose greatness by constantly affirming our direction and intent. Transformation neither comes quickly nor immediately. It's true that our sins are forgiven the moment we repent and seek forgiveness, however, the creation of our new character takes a lifetime of getting up and starting over.

At 7:00 P.M. on October 20, 1968, a few thousand spectators remained in the Mexico City Olympic Stadium. It was cool and dark. The last of the marathon runners, each exhausted, were being carried off to first-aid stations. More than an hour earlier, Mamo Wolde of Ethiopia—looking as fresh as when he started the race—crossed the finish line, the winner of the 16-mile, 385-yard event.

As the remaining spectators prepared to leave, those sitting near the marathon gates suddenly heard the sound of sirens and police whistles. All eyes turned to the gate. A lone figure wearing the colors of Tanzania entered the stadium. His name was John Stephen Akhwari. He was the last man to finish the marathon. His leg bloodied and bandaged, severely injured in a fall, he grimaced with each step. He hobbled around the 400-meter track.

The spectators rose and applauded him as if he were the winner. After crossing the finish line, Akhwari slowly walked off the field without turning to the cheering crowd.

In view of his injury and having no chance of winning a medal, someone asked him why he had not quit. He replied, "My country did not send me 7,000 miles to start the race. They sent me 7,000 miles to finish it."[28] This is the kind of perseverance we need!

A FINAL NOTE

Very few of you have met Frances Marie Flinn. I heard about Fran by way of her sister, Joanie, when we lived in Torrance, California in 1968. In 1992 it was my pleasure to personally meet Fran and hear her remarkable story. At my request she wrote it down so you can hear it, too. Perhaps you also will be struck by God's compelling persistence to redeem us, and the gentle kindness he exhibits to help us do his will.

Fran's Story

"Several years ago while returning from Palm Springs, I cried all the way home. My life was falling apart: my wages were being garnished, my car was about to be repossessed, I owed $15,000 in liens on my house, $50,000 to my ex-husband, and the remainder of my creditors seemed to want every penny I didn't have. I said, 'God, if you are really real, why did you let these things happen to me?'

"In an instant, God replayed the last twenty years of my life, reminding me of how he had delivered me from every desperate circumstance I had ever been in. My daughters at one time were in a car accident that could have taken their lives, but God mercifully spared them. And my own life was threatened nearly thirty years ago when I was attacked and nearly killed in my own home one day.

"I recalled that, as a man was beating me repeatedly over the head with an iron, God suddenly intervened. The man heard a noise at my front door and went to see what it was. In that moment I cried out, 'God, please let me live so that I can raise my daughters!' Suddenly, I heard a voice telling me what to do. He said, 'Get up, go out the back door and go two doors down for help.' With blood dripping down my face and into my eyes, I was empowered with a supernatural strength that I knew could only have come from God. I got up, and, miraculously, did exactly what the voice had told me. It so happened that a minister lived two doors down from me. He had been at church that morning, but, curiously, had forgotten a book and had returned home to get it. I appeared at his door just as he was leaving. He and another neighbor tracked down my attacker who was apprehended by the police. They then tended to my wounds.

"I knew that something supernatural had happened to me when my life was spared that day. I began my search for God. I had always avoided 'those Jesus freaks' with their smiling faces and incessant exclamations of, 'Praise the Lord!' But while watching television one day, I heard a preacher saying, 'If you don't know Jesus Christ as your personal Savior, you're fighting a losing battle.' I knew then that the choices I had made in my life, including my two divorces, had been made without ever consulting God. Now I was reaping the consequences of my own sin and rebellion. I said, 'God, if you're really real, I want to know you and serve you.'

"Walking up the steps of the South Bay Church of God in Torrance, California, I remembered how my sister Joanie and so many other faithful people had prayed for me. I remember Joanie telling me that if I would memorize and live by just one scripture, Proverbs 3:5–6, it would literally change my life. I am happy to say that I did, and it has! I do trust in the Lord with all my heart. I no longer lean on my own understanding, but now acknowledge him in all my ways and trust him to direct my path.

"Soon after my conversion I got involved with a Christian singles group where I volunteered my time and energy to provide food for their social activities. I remember praying to God, asking God what I could do to own my own business. I believe that God told me that he and I would go into the catering business, and that he would be my partner. So, keeping my full-time job as a buyer for a major supermarket chain, and with a butcher block, a slicing machine, and an ad in the yellow pages, God and I began our catering business. With the help of family and friends, I was able to keep my home and eventually pay all of my bills.

"Now, nearly thirteen years later, God and I are still partners. We have a beautiful facility with our own equipment, several faithful employees, and four vans. I own my own home. My greatest joy in life, though, is knowing that all three of my daughters know Jesus as their personal Savior and Lord.

"Though death stared me in the face, when I cried out to God he heard my cries and delivered me. I have found that he is with me in the midst of every difficulty, just like he was with Shadrach, Meshach, and Abednego in the middle of the fiery furnace. He has always delivered me out of every difficult circumstance. He will never leave us or forsake us, and we truly can do all things through Christ who strengthens us. Praise the Lord!"

QUESTIONS FOR DISCUSSION

1. React to the statement, "God's will is not something we must struggle to discern.... We are to adopt his goals for ourselves. We must apply our personal creativity, energy, and resources toward evangelizing others."

2. The author says we must be obedient. How can we obey something so inspecific as "go and make disciples of all nations"?

3. Recall a time you had to put feet on your faith, a time you had to "stop talking and start walking." Do we grow beyond this?

4. What does Dietrich Bonhoeffer's phrase "cheap grace" mean to you? How do we tend to cheapen God's grace in our everyday lives?

5. The author discusses three characteristics of this world's pattern: Depersonalization, Value assigned by Appearance, and Self-centeredness. What others would you add? Give examples.

6. Study the table that lists examples of system-kill and the mind-sets responsible for them. Create a similar table but use your own examples. Read Romans 12:1–21 and Hebrews 11 for ideas.

7. Read Fran's Story. How did Fran do God's will? How had system-kill victimized her? What encouragement do you find for your own life?

NOTES

1. Matthew 10:30
2. Amos 9:7–8
3. John 3:16–17
4. The three paragraphs preceding are drawn from S. V. McCasland, "Will of God," *Interpreter's Dictionary of the Bible*, vol. 4 (Nashville: Abingdon Press, 1962), 844–848.
5. 1 Timothy 1:12–14, italics added.
6. Matthew 28:18–20
7. 1 Corinthians 6:20
8. This story was told by the late Vic Gritzmacher
9. Matthew 22:28–32
10. James F. Colainni, editor, *Sunday Sermons Treasury of Illustrations*, Volume 2 (Pleasantville, NJ: Voicings Publications), 1982.
11. Genesis 18:12
12. Genesis 22:2
13. Genesis 22:9–10
14. Daniel 3:17–18
15. Daniel 3:28
16. Colainni, 407–408.
17. Hebrews 12:1
18. "To Illustrate," *Leadership*, (Winter 1983), 83.
19. Romans 12:1–2
20. James 2:2–4
21. Harold Myra, *Is There a Place I Can Scream?* (Garden City, NY: Doubleday & Company, Inc., 1975), 27–32.
22. Romans 12:10
23. I could not find the source of this true story.
24. Saul's story is found in 1 Samuel 9:1–31
25. Romans 12:1–2
26. Philippians 4:8–9, italics added
27. Hebrews 11:24–27, italics added
28. Wes Thompson, "Finishing Well," "To Illustrate…," *Leadership*, (Spring 1992), 49.